—— Police intervention in marital violence

—POLICE INTERVENTION IN MARITAL VIOLENCE

— *Alan Bourlet*

Open University Press
Milton Keynes • Philadelphia

Open University Press
Celtic Court
22 Ballmoor
Buckingham
MK18 1XW

and
1900 Frost Road, Suite 101
Bristol, PA 19007, USA

First Published 1990

British Library Cataloguing in Publication Data
Bourlet, Alan Robert, *1939–*
    Police intervention in marital violence.
    1. Great Britain. Battered wives. Protection. Role of
    police
    I. Title
    362.8292

    ISBN 0 335 09293 4
        0 335 09292 6 (pbk)

Library of Congress Cataloging-in-Publication Data
Bourlet, Alan, 1939–
    Police intervention in marital violence/by Alan Bourlet.
        p. cm.
    Includes bibliographical references.
    ISBN 0-335-09293-4   ISBN 0-335-09292-6 (pbk.)
    1. Wife abuse – Investigation.   2. Wife abuse – Great Britain.
    I. Title.
    HV8079.S67B68   1990
    363.2'32 – dc20   89-49163 CIP

Typeset by Vision Typesetting, Manchester
Printed in Great Britain by St Edmundsbury Press Ltd
Bury St Edmunds, Suffolk

— Contents

— Acknowledgements   vii

— Abbreviations   viii

— Introduction   ix

1 — The nature and extent of marital violence   1

2 — Police intervention   13

3 — Competing pressures   28

4 — The victim's expectations and needs   36

5 — Formulation and application of police policy   51

6 — Translating policy into practice   71

7 — Implications for the future   84

8 — The way forward   99

— References   103

— Index   107

— Acknowledgements

My special thanks are due to all those who gave their time by assisting in this study. To the patient and willing interviewers who conducted the questionnaires, often in difficult and moving circumstances. To the chief officers and their staff, who supplied policy documents, and to their officers who answered the questions so candidly. Finally, to the victims of the violence who agreed to relive their experiences in the hope that the lessons of the past might help us to avoid making the same mistakes again.

All who have participated in this study have been affected by it, or have learned its lessons, in some measure as it has touched their lives. In the words of Tennyson:

I am part of all that I have met. (*Ulysses*)

— Abbreviations

ACPO	Association of Chief Police Officers
DHSS	Department of Health and Social Security
GLC Police Group	Greater London Council Police Monitoring and Research Group
HMCIC	Her Majesty's Chief Inspector of Constabulary
NWAF	National Women's Aid Federation
RUC	Royal Ulster Constabulary
SEGS	Socio-economic Groups
Select Committee	Parliamentary Select Committee on Violence in Marriage (1975)
WNC	Women's National Commission

— Introduction

But oh, unmanlike men, and stain of your sex! Is this a point of your manhood, or any ornament of your valor, to busy yourselves for the disgrace of women, whom nature hath disarmed or corporal, and education disabled of mental courage for revenge? (Heale, 1609, quoted in Roy, 1984)

Marital violence is a subject in which all police officers have to take an interest, for it occurs far too often in their professional lives for it to be ignored. My interest in the subject had existed for many years, before being extended in 1981 when attending the first national conference on the subject at the University of Kent at Canterbury. Most police officers deal with a considerable number of 'domestics' throughout their careers and, likewise, sometimes attend domestic murders or suicides, which are often the corollary of domestic disputes. The Canterbury conference generated a fervour, notably among the Women's Aid Federation, who were very vociferous, especially in their criticism of the service given by police to women in marital violence situations. The seeds were sown that, perhaps, the police did not always deal with this thorny problem with the best interests of the victim in mind. I was (and remain) convinced that most of the police officers with whom I'd served over the previous 30 years, were compassionate individuals, who had dealt fairly and impartially with marital violence as they saw it, while at the same time witnessing the worst side of human nature. However, a nagging doubt remained, and when the opportunity arose to research the subject, with the organizer and co-ordinator of the 1981 conference as one of the supervisors, I jumped at the chance. It has often seemed to some officers, when reading criticisms of police action relating to marital violence, that the police side of the problem was not always understood. The legal and social constraints under which they operate have not always been fully explained, or explored, resulting in complaints of inaction, or, as Oppenland (1982) puts it, 'copping out'. This project gave the opportunity not only to put the police point of view, by drawing on the experiences and opinions of police officers, but it also presented the chance to gather relevant facts and to present them in a careful and objective manner.

By this method, if change were found to be necessary, it was hoped that it would come about more rapidly if the facts were to be pointed out by a member of the police service, rather than by other members of society whose motives (at least to police officers) were often suspect.

Marital violence is not some new phenomenon which has surfaced in the past few years; it has probably existed since men and women first formed close relationships. There is evidence of it stretching back thousands of years. The Romans experienced it and, indeed, the much loved Mr Punch

Figure 0.1 Punch and Judy

derives his existence from a Roman mime called 'Maccus'. This was later revived in the seventeenth century, in the story of Silvio Fiorillo, who murdered both his child and his wife (Brewer, 1978: 1019).

The morning service of the Jewish Book of Prayer contains the following prayer response for men:

> Blessed art thou, O Lord our God, King of the universe, who hast not made me a woman.

Judaism has survived for over 5000 years, and some of the ancient ideology of the dominance of men over women still remains. Women's refuges are necessary even in the modern state of Israel, as I discovered when visiting that country in November 1987.

The domination of women by men and their subordinate position has been underpinned by many cultures over the centuries. The philosophy has been worked and reworked in many areas of literature and, more recently, in the popular press and in the cinema. Even Shakespeare was not averse to the suggestion of male domination in some of his works. In *The Taming of the Shrew*, for example, Petruchio says in Act III, Scene II:

> I will be master of what is mine own. She is my goods, my chattels.

This sentiment was echoed by the man who, when a police officer intervened to stop him beating his wife, said, 'Mind your own business. She's mine and I'll do with her as I like.'

This book is not concerned with the causes of domestic violence – other researchers have covered this side of the subject in far greater depth. What it is concerned with is the intervention of the police in incidents of marital violence, and the circumstances surrounding police policies which govern and control that intervention and the actions stemming from it.

The term 'marital' itself requires definition. It should not be confined to couples who are actually married, because this would fail to take account of the many people who live together as husband and wife, although they have not actually formalized their relationship, or are not in a position to do so. In New South Wales, Australia, for example, *de facto* marriages are acknowledged in the state's marital violence legislation. This term, therefore, encompasses relationships where the partners live together for a reasonable period of time, whether they are married or not.

Although marital violence has existed for thousands of years, the police have only been involved in marital disputes since the professional police service was founded in London in 1829. From their inception, the police were seen as a force entrusted to service only the criminal law, rather than the civil law. In practice, officers do not have the powers to take any action in marital matters unless a breach of the Queen's Peace has taken place, or is thought likely to occur. A crime is, of course, a breach of the Queen's Peace and clearly can be actioned, but when victims criticize the police for inactivity, saying that they have been told to get in touch again when something concrete happens, it appears that the role of the police may be misunderstood. Little assistance can be offered before one or more of the parties moves towards committing an illegal act; the police cannot be expected to act on thoughts or intentions. Police officers have no powers of arbitration and have to be very careful when intruding into domestic situations.

As a result of the constraints on police action, a philosophy has grown up within the police service over the years that officers should be wary of becoming involved in domestic situations lest one or both of the parties should turn on the officers concerned. A further myth is that female victims of assaults are very likely to withdraw their support for a prosecution against their spouse, leaving the police in a difficult and frustrating position. So many myths and stereotypes abound, that the Women's Aid Federation (1989) has produced a leaflet entitled *Unhelpful Myths and Stereotypes about Domestic Violence*, which does much to explode them.

Much has been written in the past few years about the role of the police in marital violence. Several commentators have suggested that the police are often unsympathetic to the position of women caught up in violent relationships. Some suggest that this is representative of a service which mirrors the patriachal society in which we live. Others contend that the training of police officers and the policies under which they operate are outmoded and lacking in perception of the needs of society today.

As a police officer, I have long held the view that there are no simplistic answers to the many factors which govern the way that such incidents develop in the first place, and the manner in which they are handled by police officers. However, I saw the need to research the problem from a police point of view, as well as to try to understand how victims perceive the officers who deal with their case. Therefore, the research in this book has been directed along these lines.

1— The nature and extent of marital violence

Any attempt to categorize or define violent acts is fraught with difficulties. One person's view as to what is 'violent' may differ from that of another, and one person's tolerance of violence is, at least in part, subjective. Our perception of violence and its acceptability often depends upon the circumstances of the experience and the situation of the participants. Pahl (1985a) argues that police action often differs between similar acts of violence, depending upon whether they occur in the privacy of the home or in a public place. It may well be that some people have a higher threshold of tolerance, due to their previous experience or upbringing. On the other hand, some people may even interpret non-physical acts, such as shouting or arguing, as violent, simply because this engenders fear in them (*Woman Magazine*, 1985).

The generally accepted meaning of violence, however, and the one I shall adopt here, is the use of some degree of physical force. This may include slapping, pushing, shoving, punching, kicking, kneeing, butting, striking with or throwing household objects, the use of weapons, and any attempt to smother or strangle. Dobash and Dobash (1979) discovered that attacks usually only involve one kind of force, such as a punch, but that they sometimes involve several kinds of violence. They found the most common forms of physical abuse to be repeated punching to the face and body, followed by kicking, kneeing or butting.

At some stage in every discussion on marital violence, the question will be posed as to why researchers concentrate primarily on the violence suffered by women at the hands of men, at the apparent expense of research into similar violence against men by women. There is no denying that women occasionally injure or even kill their partners, and that some women can be as aggressive or as violent as men. Some women in the *Woman Magazine* (1985) survey admitted that they had assaulted their

1

husbands during the course of marital arguments, and one man wrote to the House of Commons Parliamentary Select Committee on Violence in Marriage in 1975 to draw attention to the fact that men are sometimes assaulted by their wives. What evidence there is, however, indicates that the problem of assaults by women on men is insignificant compared with the problem of assaults by men on women. To give a comparable amount of time to both these areas of research would, in my view, be unwarranted and wasteful.

The nature of violence

The women interviewed during the research on which this book is based (see Chapter 4) spoke of several types of violence:

1 Subject 105 was 6 months pregnant when she was run over deliberately by her husband in his lorry after an argument. She miscarried and lost the child.
2 Subject 106 had been out to visit a friend, which annoyed her husband. He beat her with his fists, causing her a broken nose, black eyes and deadened face nerves.
3 Following an argument between her husband and a male friend in the pub, subject 107's husband started an argument at home because she had been sitting with the other man. He beat her with his fists and feet, causing her two black eyes, a swollen nose and face, some hair pulled out, a foot mark on the face and a cut finger.
4 Following an argument over another woman, the husband of subject 108 assaulted her with his fists and feet, causing her broken ribs, black eyes and bruising all over.

The experiences of these women are representative of the kind of attacks reported by many other researchers.

A survey carried out by *Woman Magazine* (February 1985) stimulated a response from 'over a thousand women', all of whom indicated that they were regularly involved in serious arguments with their respective partners. More than 800 of them also spoke of violence of varying degrees being used against them in the course of these arguments, ranging from pushing and shaking, to punching, kicking and throttling. Nearly 14 per cent of those who responded had suffered broken face bones, or facial cuts and bruising. Of those women who received medical treatment, only half of them actually told the doctor how they had really come by their injuries.

During Dobash and Dobash's (1979) research in Glasgow, 109 women were interviewed, all of whom had been severely and systematically beaten by their husbands. They had experienced violence which ranged from simple physical acts, such as kicking, strangling, punching, kneeing or smothering, to the use of household objects as weapons.

Under-reporting

A major difficulty in estimating the nature and extent of marital violence is the problem of under-reporting, sometimes known as 'the dark figure'. The results of the *Woman Magazine* (1985) survey indicated that 1 in 3 of the 800 women who had suffered violence at the hands of their partner felt so isolated that there was no-one they could confide in. Of the remaining two-thirds who confided in some third person, only 28 per cent went to the police. From this survey, it can be seen that only just over 17 per cent of the cases were actually reported to the police, leaving the vast majority unreported. It is not surprising that many researchers (Edwards, 1986; Dobash and Dobash, 1979; Pahl, 1985) comment upon the inaccuracy of statistical information caused by under-reporting.

Although virtually all of the assaults in Dobash and Dobash's (1979) study were accompanied by relatively serious injuries, and therefore fell within the bounds of criminal offences, only 2 out of 98 known assaults were ever reported to the police. This experience is also confirmed by Binney *et al.* (1981) and Horley (1988). One of the major reasons given by women in Horley's study for not reporting an assault was that they did not feel that the police would be sympathetic to their individual circumstances. The Women's National Commission Report (1985) states that only 2 per cent of incidents of marital violence are reported to the police and that assault by husbands on their wives was the second most common form of violence reported to them.

It is clear, therefore, that because of under-reporting, the number of incidents where marital violence occurs and which become known to the police is only the tip of the iceberg.

Police recording practice

The inaccurate figure produced by under-reportage is further compounded by the way in which the police actually record the information that does come into their possession. When such incidents are reported, there is a widely held view in some quarters that the police do not always record them as crimes, thus reducing the worth of the figures produced. Edwards (1986) comments on under-recording by the police as follows:

> When incidents of such violence are reported, there is, too, a feeling that such incidents are under-recorded. The main problem, so far as the criminal recording process is concerned, is that unless a crime is

3

identified, such incidents, though some of them may be episodic, serious, or minor, there is no way of them being traced or checked out, no means of being logged.

Essentially, the incident has to be identified as a crime before being recorded as such. This may seem to be an over-simplified statement, but the identification of the crime is a subjective matter and open to the views, opinions and even the prejudices of individual police officers. The train of events can either be brought about by a simple statement, such as 'My husband hit me and caused this injury', or can start as a result of the officer observing the injury and deducing the circumstances from the available evidence. At this point, another factor creeps into the equation, i.e. discretion. The decision as to whether to accept the situation as a criminal offence is one for the individual officer at the scene. If he or she sees the case as one for criminal action, then the matter is recorded as such and becomes part of the local (and eventually the national) statistics. If the individual officer sees the matter as one which does not require criminal action, then the parties may only be advised to seek redress in some other way. Many researchers see this apparently unsympathetic attitude as less than helpful to the plight of women caught up in marital disputes. As Oppenland (1982) comments: 'The police are copping-out in handling family disputes.'

Some of the police officers in the Metropolitan and Kent studies described later in this book did not see intervention in marital disputes as 'real police work'. However, Pahl (1982) comments – that 'Dealing with assaults may be difficult police work, but it is nevertheless real police work.'

For an incident to become a statistic, someone has to accept the act as criminal. This is not always as simple as it may seem, and police intervention in such matters is very much bound by the criminal law, police procedures and evidential requirements. It is also affected by other features of police policy, such as resource management and the allocation of time to certain types of incidents. If the police are 'copping-out' or not regarding assaults as 'real police work', as has been suggested, how much time can they notionally devote to marital violence before the public feels that they are neglecting other areas of policing, often identified as having a higher priority? This is a debate with which I shall deal more fully in Chapter 2.

Defining the violence

The Offences Against the Person Act, 1861, is the legislation which contains the statutory offences applicable to interpersonal violence, such as injuries caused by spouses. There are four sections of the Act which are normally utilized by the police to prosecute offences of assault or of causing injury:

1 *Section 42: Common assault.* Committed by any person who shall assault and beat another. Maximum penalty: £400 fine.
2 *Section 47: Assault occasioning actual bodily harm.* Committed by any person who shall commit actual bodily harm to another. Maximum penalty: 5 years imprisonment.

    The term 'actual bodily harm' means 'any hurt or injury calculated to interfere with the health or comfort of the victim and includes an hysterical or nervous condition resulting from the assault'.
3 *Section 20: Unlawful wounding.* Committed by any person who unlawfully and maliciously wounds, or inflicts grievous bodily harm on, any person, with or without an instrument. Maximum penalty: 5 years imprisonment.

    This section is generally used for woundings where the skin is cut or broken in some way. The difference between this and the following offence is that the 'intent' to commit the injury does not have to be proved. It is sufficient to prove malice and that it was not accidental.
4 *Section 18: Grievous bodily harm.* Committed by any person who shall commit grievous bodily harm or wound any other person, *with intent* so to do. Maximum penalty: life imprisonment. The intent, either actual or implied, must be proved.

Of the offences created by The Offences Against the Person Act, 1861, it is usual for the police to take action in all except common assault cases. In such cases, the victim can take out a private summons under Section 42 of the Act or, alternatively, sue the perpetrator through the civil courts for damages. In all other cases, any prima facie evidence of the commission of an offence should result in the completion of a crime report by the police and consideration being given to criminal proceedings.

Police 'criming' in practice

It is possible for police officers, when considering the strength of evidence in support of a particular charge following an assault, to consider 'criming down'. That is to say, moving the classification of the offence down one category. Thus a Section 47 actual bodily harm can be 'crimed down' to a common assault and the victim advised to seek their own redress. Equally, woundings may also be downgraded to actual bodily harm (although, with each offence carrying a similar penalty, there is no incentive for this to be done). Edwards (1986) found evidence of 'criming down' in interviews with police officers in two areas of London, and other researchers have commented likewise. Some police forces use a rule of thumb to decide on prosecutions. One force employs a 'stitch rule', where a charge is only brought if it is necessary for the woman to receive stitches as a result of the assault. In keeping with many other forces, any lesser injuries result in the matter being treated as common assault and the woman being advised to take the matter further herself. In all such cases, no crime report is completed and the incident goes unrecorded.

Chatterton (1981) observed that bland entries such as 'Domestic dispute – parties advised as to civil remedy', can often hide quite serious injuries. The Women's National Commission (1985) noted that prosecutions following marital incidents were rare. Of those police divisions investigated, the highest rate of prosecutions was brought in Bristol (3.2%). This did not match the estimates made by the police commanders of these divisions, who thought that charges were brought in 5–20 per cent of cases. Faragher carried out a study of the Staffordshire police in 1978, with particular emphasis on marital violence. He attended 26 incidents with police officers and judged that, in 10 of them (38%), the officers could have taken criminal action against the offenders had they wished to do so. Faragher felt that although the circumstances in which charges should be brought were clearly laid down, officers frequently ignored them and used their own discretion (Faragher, 1985).

It is evident therefore, that there is both under-reporting of violent assaults by victims and under-recording by the police.

Official figures

Even the official statistics which are produced by the Home Office each year fail accurately to identify and quantify the extent of marital violence. The Parliamentary Select Committee was critical in 1975 of Home Office statistics because they did not actually identify the relationship between the victim and the person committing the offence (House of Commons Select Committee on Violence in Marriage, 1975). The four categories of criminal assault listed above do not distinguish between marital violence and other offences. Ten years later, the Women's National Commission (1985: 47) commented:

> The Working Group have noted the absence of adequate national statistics, or reported incidents of marital violence, their type, and the proportions of known violent situations which ended in the commission of life-threatening crime.

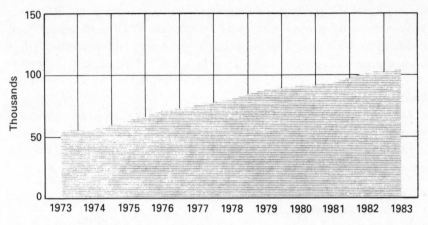

Figure 1.1 Woundings and assaults occasioning actual bodily harm (Home Office, 1983)

The only way open to us to try to quantify the extent of marital violence is to look at other indicators which can be taken as representative of the problem as a whole. Although these indicators do not give the complete picture in themselves, they are nevertheless closely linked and have to be taken as secondary evidence of the situation. The Under Secretary of State for the Welsh Office, using the limited Colchester Study (1975) as a yardstick, gave evidence to the Parliamentary Select Committee that 'there might be perhaps 5000 battered *wives* in Wales each year, out of a figure of 680 000 married women' (1971 census). In 1985, Welsh Women's Aid reported that 1055 women (plus 1747 children) were accommodated at their 24 refuges in the principality. However, not all battered women find their way to a refuge, and it is likely that the 1975 estimate is very inaccurate.

The relevant category of the Home Office statistics in which woundings and actual bodily harm offences are represented (excluding serious woundings with intent) is shown in Fig. 1.1 for the years 1973–83. It will be noted that this category of offences nearly doubled in the 10 years under review, from 54 545 in 1973, to 104 894 in 1983. Although there is no accurate means of estimating the proportion of these offences which relate to violence against women in a domestic situation, it is likely that they also increased during this period. The only evidence to support this view comes from small surveys carried out by Dobash and Dobash (1979) and McClintock (1963), which indicate that such figures are fairly constant, running at about 25 per cent of all similar offences reported to the police. It is by no means certain whether the incidence of marital violence is actually growing at the rate shown by these figures, or whether the awareness and sensitizing of the public to violent acts by groups such as the Women's Movement has ensured that more people are willing to report such incidents to the police. This awareness could have had a processing effect upon the figures, and they should not be taken at face value to show that more people are actually being injured, but simply that we are now more aware of these injuries.

Divorce is probably the main response to marital violence. Although there may be many factors which contribute towards the one essential requisite that the marriage has suffered 'irretrievable breakdown', this can only be established in law if one of five factors exist:

- adultery;
- unreasonable behaviour;
- desertion for 2 years;
- separation for 2 years, where the parties both consent; or
- separation for 5 years.

In 1980, over 150 000 divorce decrees were granted and 70 per cent of the petitioners were women. The most common grounds cited were 'unreasonable behaviour'. In this category, 89 per cent of the petitioners were women, who in practice were required to provide evidence to substantiate the extent of the 'unreasonable behaviour', usually amounting to varying degrees of violence by their husbands against them. 'Unreasonable behaviour' was cited in 33 per cent of the divorce cases in that year, i.e. nearly 50 000. According to Parker (1985), violence may well have been a factor in the other classifications shown above. The fact that adultery was alleged as the prime cause does not mean that violence was not a regular feature of the marriage; likewise, separation for 2 years, or an alleged desertion, may have been triggered by a violent episode. Dobash *et al.* (1985) discovered that many women suffered assaults for several years before seeking assistance or remedy in law. An average of 11 incidents emerged as a profile of the violent acts, with the greatest number of women seeking refuge between the fifth and tenth years of marriage. What the divorce figures hide, however, is that hundreds of thousands of incidents are likely to go undiscovered in Great Britain each year and relatively few lead to legal action and divorce.

A concomitant of divorce proceedings is the law relating to injunctions restraining a violent partner from molesting the applicant, assaulting her, or intruding into the home once he has been excluded. Prior to 1976, the only orders which could be made were interlocutory injunctions, i.e. injunctions made once legal proceedings, such as divorce or action for damages, had been commenced.

With the passing of the Domestic Violence and Matrimonial Proceedings Act, 1976, powers existed for the county courts to grant injunctions to applicants restraining the respondent from molesting them or a child living with them; excluding the respondent from the home, or specific area in which the home is included; or ordering the respondent to allow the applicant back into the home (Section 1). Section 2 of the Act permitted a county court judge to attach a power of arrest to such an injunction, if he or she were satisfied that the respondent had caused actual bodily harm to the applicant or a child concerned, and considered that he was likely to do so again. The number of injunctions and those with arrest clauses attached to them are as follows:

1981

Injunctions with power of arrest	1876
Injunctions without power of arrest	5598
Injunctions with power added	184
Applications refused	217

1983

Injunctions with power of arrest	2501
Injunctions without power of arrest	7952
Injunctions with power added	225
Applications refused	367

1984

Injunctions with power of arrest	3568
Injunctions without power of arrest	10 562
Injunctions with power added	347
Applications refused	380

1985

Injunctions with power of arrest	3314
Injunctions without power of arrest	13 020
Injunctions with power added	741
Applications refused	511

It is interesting to note that in the 4 years from 1982 to 1985, the number of injunctions issued rose by 132 per cent to 16 334. The applications refused rose from 2.90 per cent in 1982 to 3.13 per cent in 1985. Parker (1985) feels that judges themselves undermine the effectiveness of both exclusion orders and arrest clauses by attaching time limits to them. In most cases, this is only for 3 months, but at the end of this time, a woman has to ask the court for a renewal. Secondly, Parker suggests that the judiciary are split as to what evidence is required for a man to be excluded, often requiring more than the Act appears to specify. Thirdly, before a power of arrest is attached, judges again require evidence that actual bodily harm has been caused. In *McClaren* v *McClaren*, 1979, a power of arrest was removed from the order because the judge had not taken evidence that actual bodily harm had been caused to the applicant.

A further power to grant protection orders, similar in many respects to county court injunctions, exists in the Domestic Proceedings and Magistrates' Courts Act, 1978. The 'personal protection order' granted under the Act can take the place of a county court injunction, in that an exclusion order can be made and a power of arrest can also be attached to it. Clearly, the threat of violence is a constituent factor in such applications and may be used as yet another indicator of the measure of violence suffered by women who are married or cohabiting. The figures for personal protection orders for 1982–4 are as follows:

- 1982: total, 8680; arrest clause, 2280 (26.27%).
- 1983: total, 7740; arrest clause, 2020 (26.10%).
- 1984: total, 8480; arrest clause, 2090 (24.65%).

These figures are not the final indicators of the situation and have to be seen in the context of the whole problem. However, they do indicate the scale of marital violence, and it is a real and manifestly serious problem which appears to be growing. Clearly, the need to examine the other indicative information would not be necessary if the recommendations of the Parliamentary Select Committee had been followed and Home Office statistics were made to link the relationship between victim and assailant (House of Commons Select Committee on Violence in Marriage, 1975). This information is relatively easy to gather, especially now that electronic and computer systems are more readily available to assist in its compilation. Similar information is available, for example, in relation to the statistics for homicides in England and Wales. The statistics for the 10 years 1973–83 are shown in Fig. 1.2.

Were such figures available in relation to woundings and actual bodily harm offences, as recommended by the Select Committee in 1975, the extent of the problem could not only be monitored on a yearly basis, it could also be monitored on a geographical basis, especially by those police forces whose offence codings are available down to parish level. The ability to identify those areas where there is an apparently high incidence of domestic injuries, together with a knowledge of the times and days of the week when violence occurs, would enable the social services, the probation service, local authority housing services, the police and several other

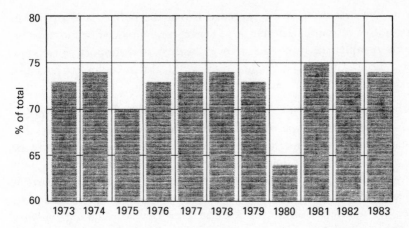

Figure 1.2 The number of homicides where the victim is acquainted with the suspect

agencies to assess their policies and resources in relation to this problem, and possibly allow them to make provision to deal more effectively with it. Instead, we have to rely on estimates to gauge the responses given to the parties involved in these disputes. Whereas the Commissioner of Police for the Metropolis estimated that nearly 40 per cent of all recorded offences of violence against the person in London in 1984 resulted from domestic incidents, he was relying on fairly imprecise information on which to base this assumption. Given the level of under-reporting and under-recording, the Commissioner still does not have an accurate system, with national reporting standards, from which to draw his conclusions (Commissioner of Police for the Metropolis, 1984).

What can be concluded from the evidence available, as uncertain as it is, is that marital violence has assumed considerable proportions over the past few years and the indications are that it is still growing. It is becoming more and more apparent as each year passes that the views of the Select Committee and the Women's National Commission should be implemented and full statistics be kept. There is so much anecdotal evidence concerning the frightful injuries inflicted upon women, that one eventually becomes almost bored with the repetitive nature of them. The *Woman Magazine* study produced some plaintive cries for help from some of the respondents, many of whom had endured such treatment for years. Some of the women in this and other studies felt that the police officers who had dealt with them were unsympathetic. The attitudes, training, experience and indeed the prejudices of the police all play an important part in the way women perceive the assistance they receive from the police. The Women's National Commission (1985: 49) commented:

...so the first myth to be exploded is that the police have a uniform attitude or response to domestic violence. It may indeed be the case that some complainants may get a very sensitive, and supportive response from police; in other cases they may well feel that the police have not taken their complaint seriously.

Whatever the truth of the matter may be, and however the police themselves and women perceive the role of the police, the fact remains that in many sections of society the distinct impression exists, rightly or wrongly, that the police do not deal sensitively and resolutely with serious domestic assaults. The reasons for this are manifold, and serious research is needed in order to unearth the true situation, as well as the cause and its remedy. The Select Committee held the same view after taking evidence from many sources and the need appears to persist today.

2— Police intervention

As was mentioned in Chapter 1, it is difficult to identify some of the problems related to marital violence, simply because we are unsure of their scale. Without accurate official figures, it is impossible to ascertain whether injuries arising from marital violence are actually increasing at the same rate as other crimes, thereby hindering chief police officers from planning their responses and allocating their resources accordingly. To quote the memorandum of the Metropolitan Police to the Select Committee:

> The full scope of the problem of battered wives must of necessity be speculative. (House of Commons Select Committee on Violence in Marriage, 1975: 375)

Nor is it always possible for chief officers to know with accuracy where such assaults have occurred or are likely to occur, thereby preventing the implementation and encouragement of special provisions or policies of prevention.

This chapter seeks to explore the factors which shape, mould and, in some cases, constrain police action in marital violence. The perceptions the police have of their own role in this matter are also examined, as well as those of other groups and individuals having an interest in the rights and welfare of women. Police activities are displayed against the backdrop of both the criminal and civil codes of law, within which all law enforcement agencies must be seen to operate in a democratic society.

One aspect of the approach of the police to marital violence is the implementation of individual force policies, which in turn have been shaped by the criminal and civil codes of law, the rules of evidence required by these codes and the perception by the police of their own role within society as a whole. All these factors serve to keep the status quo in a state of dynamic tension, influenced only occasionally by pressure from groups in

13

society which mould and develop public and government opinion. In questions relating to marital violence, several kinds of influence may be brought to bear from groups such as the press, feminists, and some political parties. The process, it is suggested, which is generally one of evolution rather than revolution, maintains a state of equilibrium in what is otherwise one of change. Alderson (1980a) examined the issue of change in relation to the policies of chief constables. He states that:

> In a democracy, society evolves through competing pressures which motivate the political processes. Police systems sometimes have to give gently to some pressures whilst at the same time standing firm against excesses.

Alderson's choice of words is interesting, because he talks later in the same article of a 'delicate balance' in relation to giving 'gently to some pressures' and of the 'inevitable compromise' that chief constables must make in adjusting their priorities to suit the demands of such factions.

How the police perceive their role

The Women's National Commission Report indicated that there was no uniform attitude or response by the police to the problem of marital violence. They noted, however, that the police were 'reluctant to "interfere" in domestic incidents', believing that this was historically well substantiated (Women's National Commission, 1985). It is a widely held view, both inside and outside the police service today, that there is a reluctance on the part of many officers to become involved in marital disputes. This so-called 'reluctance' is apparent in a great deal of the evidence given by members of the police service to the Select Committee on Marital Violence (1975). The attitude of the service is probably best summarized by a comment contained in the memorandum of the Association of Chief Police Officers to the Select Committee, which observed:

> Whilst such problems take up considerable police time during say, 12 months, in the majority of cases the role of the police is a negative one. We are, after all, dealing with persons 'bound in marriage', and it is important, for a host of reasons, to maintain the unity of the spouses. Precipitate action by the police could aggravate the position to such an extent as to create a worse situation than the one they were summoned to deal with. The 'lesser of two evils' principle is often a good guideline in these situations. (House of Commons Select Committee on Violence in Marriage, 1975)

It will be seen, therefore, that the approach of chief officers to this problem in 1975 was one of caution, erring perhaps on the side of doing too little, rather than too much. The reasons for them taking this kind of line are many and varied. Historically, police officers have always been cautioned against interfering in matrimonial disputes. The Bristol City Police Instruction book of 1880 carried the following advice:

> The police are not to interfere unnecessarily between a man and his wife who are quarrelling, and unless it is absolutely necessary to prevent serious violence to either party or public disturbance.

Apart from the overall tenor of this advice, there are two key words contained in the paragraph essential to our understanding of these instructions today, i.e. 'serious' and 'public' – insignificant on their own, but important in the context of the shaping of police policies. The word 'serious' can be seen in the context of the 'stitch rule' (see p. 6), and the word 'public' can be viewed against the assertions of commentators such as Pahl (1985a) and Dobash *et al.* (1985), that the police are really maintaining a double standard of actions over identical incidents which occur in the privacy of the home or in public. This view was later reinforced by the East Sussex Police Code, issued in 1900:

> The police should not interfere in domestic quarrels unless there is ground to fear that actual violence is imminent. If the parties are creating any obstruction, or attracting a crowd of persons, they should be cautioned before the law is enforced.

In this case, the instruction advises action only when the incident occurs in a public place, thereby attracting general attention and a possible breach of the peace.

The Liverpool City Police Instructions of 1926 carried the matter further:

> You may enter anywhere, and even break in for the purpose of preventing a felony or serious breach of the Peace, for instance if you hear cries of 'Murder', 'Rape' or the like, or hear noises which lead you to believe that a prize fight is going on. But you must be very careful how you do this, very often people cry out a good deal before they are hurt, and, if you interfere when there is no need, especially between husband and wife, you will find that both will turn on you.

It is perhaps little wonder, then, that police officers over the last century have developed a certain ideological caution, which still persists today. This kind of advice has worked and reworked the myths that the police should

15

Figure 2.1 'The Bottle' by George Cruikshank (1847) 'You will find that both will turn on you.'

not interfere in disputes between husband and wife unless it can be avoided; that both parties may turn upon the officers concerned; and that the police should only intervene when serious injury has occurred, or is imminent, or the matter has spilled out into the public domain. This is how many police officers still perceive their role in relation to marital disputes, including those which involve violence. 'Copping out' or 'not real police work' perhaps (to quote Oppenland, 1982 and Pahl, 1982), but these policies have been reinforced by decades of experience and passed on by generations of police officers to the recruits who will take their place in the front line of operational police work.

The Working Party on Police Probationer Training (1971) reported upon the need for some form of training to assist uniformed police officers to determine the best course of action to take when dealing with domestic disturbances in the home. Young officers in particular had commented upon the complexities of some of the situations which they had encountered, and they felt that their youth and inexperience left them ill-equipped to deal with many of them (English, 1986). Until July 1989, the initial police training course (which all recruits to the police service attend) carried the following lesson notes for the guidance of officers:

1) A Domestic dispute is generally a breakdown in day to day domestic family relationships, which have reached a stage where police attendance is required.
2) There is usually no criminal offence involved and although the dispute may be an isolated occasion, it is common for some disputes to occur regularly over a long period. Police Objectives: The object of police attendance at the scene of a domestic dispute is to restore the peace. (Home Office, 1986a)

This brief written advice, together with any verbal advice given by police instructors at the training school, was probably the last formal instruction received by recruits before being posted to an operational division. It is also likely that these recruits would have received no further advice before dealing with their first real incident of marital violence. This advice does not contain information on the many complicated factors often found at the heart of such an event, or the great tact usually required when dealing with the aftermath of a breakdown between partners. It is also interesting that the notes suggest that 'There is usually no criminal offence involved...', giving the impression that this was not a major consideration in such incidents, whereas other commentators suggest that this is central to the whole issue (Pahl, 1985a; Edwards, 1986; Binney *et al.*, 1981).

Initial training notes such as these are, of course, reinforced by counselling and further advice from supervisory officers and tutor constables who guide and advise constables through their probationary period. It is probably at this stage that the dominant ideologies of street-wise, older officers are brought to bear on the attitudes of probationers. By the constant reinforcement and underpinning of these philosophies, ideas become institutionalized and adopted as grass-roots working practices and theories. These ideologies are still abroad in my experience, and are reminiscent of the advice given in some of the nineteenth- and early twentieth-century police orders mentioned earlier. Most of the officers interviewed in the limited Rochester project (see Chapter 6) disliked dealing with domestic disputes which involved marital violence. The majority felt that they were frustrating incidents to deal with, as they were often part of a repetitive series and difficult to resolve satisfactorily. (A fuller analysis of this is dealt with in Chapters 6 and 7.)

In a study conducted in the South Wales Constabulary during 1987 and 1988, 10 per cent of the 1400 assaults on police officers which occurred during that period stemmed from domestic disputes (South Wales Constabulary, unpublished). In America, where access to firearms is much easier, there is great concern regarding the serious injuries and even deaths suffered by police officers when dealing with this kind of incident (McConaghy, 1976).

Discretion

One concept which is central to the whole understanding of the police approach to marital violence is that of discretion. The decision whether or not to initiate action against the assailant is critical to the way in which the matter will be viewed from that moment on. It was on this basis that the Association of Chief Police Officers built their case in their evidence to the Select Committee in 1975, and it is still very much the linch-pin of the argument today, having drawn a recommendation from the Women's National Commission that police officers 'should not use their own discretion' when considering violence in the home (Women's National Commission, 1985: recommendation 18(iv)).

In dealing with marital violence, police officers use their judgement when deciding whether or not to commence criminal proceedings against a person. In Chapter 1, it was suggested that considerable under-recording takes place in this particular area of police work, implying that this was due to an over-emphasis on discretion. At the level of operational practices, police officers may use their powers in many different ways, from using the power of arrest, to simply giving advice or handing out a caution not to do something again. When this occurs, the officer is clearly using his or her discretion. A police officer must judge, for example, when he or she fears that a 'breach of the peace' may take place and, having judged the situation thus, has to decide whether or not to invoke the powers which are available. As the originator of legal action, the officer has considerable powers. These powers are not to be used indiscriminately, but in the pursuit of well-defined ends. The Royal Commission on the Police (1962) defined the purposes of the police thus:

> The police of this country are the instrument for enforcing the rule of law; they are the means by which civilised society maintains order, that people may live safely in their homes and go freely about their lawful business. Basically their task is the maintenance of the Queen's Peace – that is, the preservation of law and order. Without this there would be anarchy. Policemen, like everybody else, are accountable to the law. They are also the law's agents: and the uniformed policeman has for many years been recognised and accepted as the embodiment of the law's authority. In a general sense it can be said that the purpose of the police is unchanging. The constable is, as Wordsworth described the peace officer of his day, a 'Staid guardian of the public peace'.

As agents of the law, as well as being subject to the law, police officers are in a unique position. As agents, they are in a different position to that of ordinary citizens and clearly must have 'original authority' under the law to decide best how the law shall be administered in any given situation. The police are required to enforce the law, but as Scraton (1982) says, '... nothing requires them to enforce all of the law, all of the time'.

The Royal Commission's definition of the purpose of the police embraces all aspects of the law, especially the criminal law, which is constitutionally constructed under the concept of maintaining the 'Queen's Peace'. Clearly, it would be impossible for the same degree of enforcement to be paid to every minute aspect of the criminal law; police resources are, after all, finite.

In a paper prepared for a Workshop in Edinburgh on 'Discretionary Decision Making', discretion was defined as follows:

> A public official has discretion whenever the effective limits of his power leave him free to make a choice among many possible courses of action and inaction. (Davis, 1971)

Discretion, therefore, allows the person in authority to choose whether or not to take a certain course of action. It also allows a choice between the options available and the degree of action seen as necessary in the circumstances. To a constable seeking to resolve a domestic dispute or an episode of marital violence, the range of options available may be narrow, but they still exist and are available at the officer's discretion. The actual choice which is made may have a profound effect on the future relationship between the two parties concerned and, of course, in the way in which the matter is regarded, both by the police and other agencies in the future.

Alternatively, discretion operates at higher levels within a police force. What a chief officer has to decide is which aspects of the law he will concentrate upon in the particular area he polices: Should he attempt to eradicate prostitution or enforce drugs laws? Should he try to reduce burglary or petty crime, while trying to find sufficient resources to carry out these policies? Does he have sufficient left over to police a football match or supervise a protest march? He has to bear in mind the wishes of the public in the area for which he is responsible. He is accountable to his police authority (although not under their control) and has the responsibility for running his force in an efficient and effective manner. As Scraton (1982) points out, the campaign by James Anderton, Chief Constable of Greater Manchester Police, against pornography in that city in the early part of 1981, was seen by many as a 'moral crusade' rather than an attempt to prioritize a serious public problem. In direct contrast to that experience, an attempt by a member of the public to force the Commissioner of Police for the Metropolis to take action against alleged unlawful gaming in clubs in London failed, because it was not seen by the Commissioner as a policing priority in that particular area of the Metropolis. The Court of Appeal upheld the discretionary powers of a chief officer to decide upon policing levels and actions in his area (*R* v *Metropolitan Police Commissioner, ex parte Blackburn*, 1968).

As Goldstein (1963) says about the question of police discretion:

Police decisions not to invoke the criminal process largely determine the outer limits of law enforcement. By such decisions, the police define the ambit of discretion throughout the process of other decision makers – prosecution, grand jury, judge, probation officer, correction authority and parole and pardon boards. These police decisions, unlike their decisions to invoke the law, are generally of extremely low visibility and consequently are seldom subject to review.

The question which may now be posed is: 'How much police time could or should actually be expended on domestic disputes and marital violence?' This is dependent to a certain extent upon the amount of public sympathy and support such a deployment of resources would command, especially if other areas of policing were to be deprived of police attention as a result.

Because of its low public profile, marital violence is unlikely to figure high on the list of priorities of chief police officers, unless some of the pressures about which Alderson (1980a) wrote are applied to persuade chief police officers that marital violence should have a higher priority and, therefore, a greater slice of the resources cake.

In the South Wales Constabulary in 1987, a total of 20 311 'domestic disputes' were referred to the police for assistance. This definition includes matters other than marital violence, but even if allowance is made for disputes which did not come within my own definition of marital violence, it can be seen that many thousands of marital disputes arose which required the commitment of police resources, and many of them are likely to have involved violence. The Women's National Commission (1985) heard evidence that 'wife assault' was the second most common form of violence known to the police, accounting for 25 per cent of all recorded violent crime.

In his annual report for 1988, Her Majesty's Chief Inspector of Constabulary (Home Office, 1989) does not once mention marital violence in his review of the year's events, traditionally considered of importance to the police. Public order situations, crime, drugs misuse and terrorism are all touched upon, but the allocation of resources for marital violence is not featured under the headings of crime or social factors, indicating the low priority attached to marital violence by the police service.

Discipline in the police service

It should not be overlooked that the police service, unlike many other professions, is subject to a strict code of conduct, which contains penalties ranging from admonishment to dismissal from the force, with chief officers being able to fine their officers or reduce them in rank, if they think it appropriate. Although a police officer may have 'original authority' in actioning criminal proceedings, he or she may face being disciplined for taking the wrong kind of action or, in some circumstances, for neglecting to do anything at all. It should be no surprise, therefore, if some police officers were to take the view that the 'lesser of two evils principle', as suggested by the Association of Chief Police Officers, should be followed in an uncertain, imprecise area such as marital violence. Many officers clearly take the view that they do not wish to interfere in the private areas of marriage and the home, especially when they may subject themselves to the risks of legal or disciplinary action at a later date. Taylor (1986), speaking as senior chaplain to the Metropolitan Police, observed:

The Police Force has a hierarchical structure and a discipline code which is often, rightly or wrongly, feared by police officers to be Draconian in operation. The individual officer will see his or her future progress in the Force in terms of passing examinations, in never making an error of judgement administratively or operationally, in having a good clean annual qualification report, in keeping clear of the medical branch and certainly not breaching the Discipline Code which could block promotion prospects or, if serious, end a career.

Therefore, some officers may subscribe to such a philosophy by keeping out of trouble, while at the same time trying to work hard and give good service. For if the matter is not noteworthy enough to be mentioned in the Chief Inspector of Constabulary's Report, why should an individual officer make marital violence his or her own crusade?

The police service, like most other services or vocations, has its own distinctive ethos, jargon and infrastructure, but, unlike others, it is highly conspicuous and its actions are subject to the greatest scrutiny, by the press and the public alike.

Not only is it necessary to understand the ideology which constructs the perceptions the police have of their role in marital situations, it is also necessary to understand how the police see their duty with regard to the law. Many commentators have been critical of police inaction in this area of their work. However, what is not always understood, is what powers and responsibilities the police actually have and how they feel these should be applied in relation to the 1962 Royal Commission on the Police.

Application of the criminal law

The police see their actions as constrained by the criminal law of this country, and quite rightly so. Under English law, the police do not have unrestricted powers in the discharge of their duties. The courses of action open to them in domestic situations are considerably restricted by statute and common law. Unlike some foreign forces, the British police are constrained by the law and must work strictly within its provisions. Although discretion is allowed for, it is a discretion based upon the right to do nothing, rather than the right to ignore legal provision (Bottomley, 1973). The criminal law of England and Wales is based upon the theoretical construct known as the 'Queen's Peace' (hence justices of the peace). This may be defined as 'The state of public tranquillity which has reigned since time immemorial.' As it is the role of the monarch, in conjunction with Parliament, to make laws which will assist in preserving this state of tranquillity or 'peace', so any offence against this state is seen as an offence against the common good, or as a breach of this peace. Put another way, the commission of any criminal offence is seen as offending against the interests of the Crown and therefore against the interests of society as a whole. The criminal law, it may be said, serves the common interest and not just that of the immediate parties involved. Any offence against the criminal law is an offence against the common interest, and therefore subject to sanctions imposed in the common good.

When the Metropolitan Police was established in 1829, the first joint commissioners, Mayne and Rowan (who were both incidentally justices of the peace), laid down the cardinal principles under which the officers of that force would operate and function:

> It should be understood at the outset, that the object to be attained is the prevention of crime. To this great end every effort of the police is to be directed. The security of person and property and the preservation of a police establishment will thus be better effected than by the detection and punishment of the offender after he has succeeded in commiting crime. He [the constable] will be civil and obliging to all people of every rank and class. He must be particularly cautious not to interfere idly or unnecessarily in order to make a display of his authority: when required to act, he will do so with decision and boldness: on all occasions he may expect to receive the fullest support in the proper exercise of his authority. He must remember that there is no qualification so indispensable to a police officer as a perfect command of temper, never suffering himself to be moved in the slightest degree by any language or threats that may be used: if he do his duty in a quiet and determined manner, such conduct will probably excite the well-disposed of the bystanders to assist him, if he requires them. In the novelty of the present establishment, particular care is to be taken that the constables of the police do not form false notions of their duties and powers. (quoted in Critchley, 1978)

Kiralfy (1967) observes that the police service has always seen these principles as the guiding precepts within which it operates, despite changes in the contemporary detail of policing and perceived priorities. It is the role of the police, therefore, to ensure that the Queen's Peace is maintained and preserved – and this applies to all criminal matters. Criminal proceedings are taken through the criminal courts of this country and any penalties are generally enforced by the sentences handed down by the courts, and by the police or prison authorities. The objectives of the criminal law are to prevent crime and punish criminals.

What must be carefully considered by all who would exhort the police to greater action, is that they '*do not* form false notions of their duties and powers' (Mayne and Rowan, 1829, quoted in Critchley, 1978).

Application of the civil law

The civil law of this country may be defined as law affecting the rights of individuals or corporate bodies. Whereas criminal law is founded on the principle of the Queen's Peace and the common good, so civil law is founded on the principle of equity and natural justice for individuals before the law. Civil law, like criminal law is enshrined in common law, as well as statute. Civil proceedings are taken in order to assist *individuals* to recover property, or to enforce obligations made in their favour (Kiralfy, 1967).

Judgments in civil cases are enforced by orders of the civil courts, which, in turn, are usually enforced by officers of those courts and not – in general – by the police. Police officers do not, as a rule, have jurisdiction in civil matters, unless specifically directed to do certain things by those courts. Most acts which occur within a marriage would fall within the civil law, and that is also where the remedy for any individual should lie should they wish to take action to redress any wrong.

The boundaries between criminal and civil law are not always clear-cut, and aspects of one often link closely with the other. Civil law has largely been created in response to pressure from below, some person or persons having suffered material loss through the act or omission of another. Criminal law, on the other hand, is imposed from above, in that Parliament observes a need to provide sanctions against an act which it deems to be against the public interest. One area of interest to this study, which represents an overlapping of both criminal and civil law, is the enforcement of injunctions made under the Domestic Violence and Matrimonial Proceedings Act, 1976. Although this Act provides for injunctions being made in the civil courts, it is possible for an arrest clause to be added by those courts, giving powers to the police to arrest a person who appears to have breached the injunction. Although such powers are seldom included in statutes, it is clearly sensible for them to be provided where a spouse will not refrain from violent or threatening actions towards the other party.

The police, while seeking to maintain the criminal law, are simultaneously subject to the provisions of the civil law, i.e. if an officer uses his or her powers to take action against an individual in an attempt to uphold the criminal law and that action is deemed in itself to have exceeded the powers provided by the criminal law, then the action becomes a matter between the two individuals (i.e. the police officer and the suspect) and a remedy may be sought by the 'suspect' against the police officer under the civil law.

A police officer, having the responsibility for his or her own actions, is still acting as an individual in the eyes of the civil law, and he or she is answerable to that law if those actions are *ultra vires*. Any claim for damages may properly be made against the officer and, generally, against his or her chief officer. By the same token, chief constables are answerable in the civil courts of this country for their own actions and those of their officers. Mark (1979) commented:

> The fact that the British police are answerable to the law, that we act on behalf of the community and not under the mantle of government, makes us the least powerful, the most accountable and therefore the most acceptable police force in the world.

This is not to pretend that the police do not stand in a special position before the eyes of the law. Not only do they observe the law, they also apply it: it is in their keeping. For example, they take many initiatives daily which utilize their special powers under the criminal law – stopping and searching suspects for drugs-related or stolen property offences, directing traffic or regulating public processions. They are always subject to the risk of civil action if they make mistakes in the application of these powers. Byford (Home Office, 1986b), commenting in his annual report as Her Majesty's Chief Inspector of Constabulary, refers to the 'ever increasing public scrutiny, often leading to demands for additional safeguards against the abuse or misuse of powers'.

Other perceptions of the police role

Not unexpectedly, other commentators see the police role in marital violence in a different way. Binney *et al.* (1981), in their study of women in refuges, discovered that more women had contacted the police than any other agency, but as many as 64 per cent had not found the police helpful. The most frequent complaint was that the police were unwilling to intervene because it was a 'domestic dispute'. Pahl (1982) observed that the categorization of an incident by police as a 'domestic dispute' tended to trivialize it, just as though 'litter' were used to describe all waste, ranging from toffee papers to industrial effluent.

The self-styled Greater London Council Police Committee (1986) commented on the role of the police in violence against women thus: 'The police treatment of rape victims and response to domestic violence has often been far from satisfactory.' It suggested that what was required was 'a critical examination and review of the attitudes of the police, barristers, judges and the law itself on domestic violence'. The Womens' Committee

Support Unit of the GLC went so far as to say that many groups feel 'that they need protection from the police, for example, rape victims and prostitute women are often justified in feeling this'.

The police sometimes fall back upon lack of powers of entry into private premises, which can affect the way in which marital violence is dealt with. 'The Englishman's home is his castle' is still a cherished concept in popular terminology in this country, and no police officer should seek to take those 'false powers and notions', to which Rowan and Mayne referred, by attempting to increase those powers without the sanction of Parliament. Pahl (1982) makes the point that police have the power to enter private premises if they fear that a serious offence is about to be committed, but seem more willing to invoke the 'privacy' and the 'sanctity' of the home in domestic situations, than when other more clear-cut criminal offences are involved.

The Younger Committee (Home Office, 1972), in its report on privacy, said:

> We have conceived the right of privacy as having two main aspects. The first of these is freedom from intrusion upon oneself, one's home, family and relationships. The second is privacy of information, that is the right to determine for oneself how and to what extent information about oneself is communicated to others.

Clearly, police intervention in marital situations may be seen by some as an intrusion into that privacy to which Younger referred. The 10 per cent of injuries in the study of assaults on police to which I referred earlier in this chapter is evidence of such an attitude, and a police officer may well fail in a claim for damages if a court takes the view that the officer was trespassing at the time of the assault.

Faragher (1985) sees the police as but one element of a legal system that 'as a whole consigns the problem of marital violence to a status of relative unimportance'. Faragher further noted from his observations with the Staffordshire Police that officers often did not carry out an arrest in some cases, even though the mandate for doing so was clearly laid down in the standing instructions issued by their own force.

Johnson (1985) saw the police role being divided into two categories, that of law enforcement and keeping the peace. He interprets police intervention in domestic situations as part of the peace-keeping role, and identifies this as inclined towards reconciliation rather than prosecution. This squares with the cautious role model put forward by the Association of Chief Police Officers (ACPO) to the Select Committee in 1975, in that the spokesman for ACPO dwelt upon the idea of the bond between husband and wife and the need to reconcile wherever possible.

The Women's National Commission Report (1985) concluded that force instructions about arrest are sometimes ignored, despite injuries to wives. Furthermore, wives were also asked if they wished to press charges arising from those injuries while in the presence of their partners. The Working Party was minded to call for criminal action to be taken, even though the act occurred 'behind closed doors'. This thinking closely followed Faragher's (1985) observations in this respect. The Commission also received evidence from several sources of police officers being 'ill-informed about what to do, and sluggish to act, even where powers of arrest exist'.

It seems apparent, therefore, that the perception by the police of their own role is often at variance with that of other individuals and bodies concerned about the question of violence towards women. Furthermore, despite having the power to act, the police are often reluctant to use that power. The police see their actions constrained by the law, by a lack of resources and, to some extent, by a certain societal consent for their cautious approach. This is one result of the concept of discretion, a concept which drew a recommendation from the Women's National Commission (1985: recommendation 18(iv)):

> Senior officers should be concerned to ensure that, where Force Instructions require this, officers should undertake arrest of persons perpetrating violence in the home, and should not use their own discretion.

By removing the element of discretion when considering a violent act, police officers would not be in a position to exercise their own judgement in such cases. Whether this would lead to more acquittals, more ready admission to bail and a greater reluctance than now to 'downgrade' injuries, only practical experience of such a system would show. One principle which must be resolved before discretion or 'original authority' is removed, is who will ultimately be responsible for the arrest if the police officer's actions are prescribed, with no room for discretionary action?

3 — Competing pressures

The role of the police in disputes between partners is almost invariably one of crisis intervention. People rarely call the police themselves until the situation has got beyond their control; and neighbours usually call them when the violence or the argument has become a cause for concern for those around. Any crisis intervention service will almost inevitably attract criticism from some quarter or other. When passions run high, it is very easy for one of the parties to become irrational and for their perception of circumstances to become warped and unbalanced. The limited powers possessed by the police to intervene in more minor disputes, as well as their ability to exercise discretion, are often misunderstood, or even misrepresented by some commentators or groups. For several years, criticisms have been levelled at the police by individuals and organizations dealing with violence against women, suggesting an unsympathetic and often antipathetic approach by them to this problem. Radical feminists and social researchers have repeatedly urged the police to make a more active response. As Hanmer et al. (1989) observe, 'Violence against women is a specific example of a more general failure in effective responses to interpersonal crime by the police.'

Clearly, the response of the police to domestic violence raises fundamental questions both about the nature of the problem and about the functions of the police. Furthermore, it raises questions about the criminal and civil codes of law and their ability to protect women from the aggression and violence levelled at them by men. Within the structure of the law and the legal process, remains the central issue of the discretion vested in the police whether to initiate criminal action against an assailant or not.

My research was set up in 1985 to examine the competing pressures which serve to influence this area of marital violence. It addressed several of the issues which have assumed importance over the past few years, the first of which was the policies of chief officers which are embodied in their force instructions (sometimes known as 'force orders'). From these it was possible to compare and contrast individual force instructions and also to discern similarities and disparities between different forces, leading to various hypotheses as to why some chief officers place a higher priority on dealing with marital violence than others. When viewing these policies and evaluating them, it is useful to bear in mind that nowhere is the role of the police in marital disputes specified and, as Pahl (1982) comments, 'In most "domestic disputes" therefore, the job of the police appears somewhat ambiguous.'

It was felt that a study of force policies carried out by a serving police officer would produce information which would have been denied to other researchers. In a study in West Yorkshire, for example, even when police cooperation was forthcoming, force policy documents were kept from those involved. Hanmer *et al.* (1989) comment: 'These orders are confidential to the force and were not revealed to the researchers...'.

Coupled with the first part of this inquiry was the additional question of what influences police policy making, so far as it relates to chief officers. The ways those policies are changed and amended and the pressures which could bring about such changes are of considerable interest to those hoping for change.

The second part of this study looked at the attitudes and perceptions of operational police officers who regularly deal with marital violence, for it is they who have to translate policy into practice, while at the same time operating within both the civil and criminal codes of law. The critical issue of discretion was explored in this part of the study and it was interesting to note how policy and practice compared with each other at that point where policy actually becomes practice. Some independent research has been carried out inside police forces over the past few years, in an attempt to understand the factors which the police take into account when deciding on the course of action they will adopt in cases of marital violence, as well as the ethos and philosophy which govern their actions (e.g. Faragher, 1985; Edwards, 1986). It is useful to compare and contrast the analysis of other commentators with the views expressed by some of Faragher's and Edwards' interviewees. Whereas Faragher's work was based upon personal observations, that of Edwards was drawn from structured interviews with police officers. Utilizing the same interview team which conducted a similar study into the Metropolitan Police on behalf of that force's Working Party on Domestic Violence, identical interviews were carried out in an area of the Kent Police Force. By setting up this project, it was possible to compare attitudes in the Metropolitan Police with those in a provincial police force, while at the same time extrapolating the Metropolitan results where they appeared similar to those of Kent.

The final part of the study was designed to look into the views of women who themselves were victims of marital violence. Another study of 42 women in Women's Aid refuges in 1981 concluded that – 'the police emerged as the least helpful of all the main agencies to which the women turned for help before going to a refuge' (Pahl, 1982).

In some areas of the UK, the relationship between the police and womens' organizations, such as the Women's Aid Federation, had become strained and cooperation between the two organizations had deteriorated to a point where the service to victims could have suffered. In one critical document, Montgomery and Bell (1985) highlighted the shortcomings which they suggested existed in the way the Royal Ulster Constabulary dealt with marital violence. This report was prepared without the participation or the cooperation of the RUC, and very little positive information on the actions of the police is contained in it.

As part of this research, the cooperation of the Women's Aid Federation was sought and freely given by several branches of that organization. The interviewers were made welcome in refuges and, furthermore, the staff of some refuges also agreed to run the questionnaires in respect of victims in those refuges. One result of this relationship was a joint conference which took place at Llandrindod Wells in November 1986, between the four Welsh police forces and all the affiliated branches of Welsh Women's Aid. This conference led to an exchange of attitudes and a much better understanding of the policies and problems of the two organizations involved. It also provided a focal point for movement towards increased liaison and an improved service to victims in Wales (Welsh Office, 1987).

One area of interest which the study addressed was whether the suggested unsympathetic approach of the police in cases of marital violence was a condition found in other crimes of a similar nature but which are committed in a public place. Some commentators have suggested that the same circumstances which would attract arrest for violence offences committed in public, do not attract the same action when committed in private. Montgomery and Bell (1985) carried out an analysis of additional factors which various researchers had found were the necessary adjuncts to attract arrest in cases of marital violence. These included:

- violence which is particularly severe;
- when the man has been drinking; and
- when the neighbours complained, or the man contested or confronted police authority.

International aspects of marital violence

An examination of the literature on domestic and marital violence reveals the international dimension of the discussion and research which has taken place over the past decade. Connors' work for the Commonwealth Secretariat (Connors, 1987) revealed that spousal violence was common in over 60 Commonwealth countries. Also pilot studies in Minneapolis, London, Ontario and New South Wales also point the way to other approaches and policies which have some place in contemporary thinking and good working practices. The study took place against the backdrop of this knowledge, which had to be taken into account when considering future policy.

Attitudes and perceptions of operational police officers

The second research strategy was designed to explore the attitudes and perceptions of randomly selected police officers who regularly dealt with incidents of marital violence. The easiest means of achieving this would have been for me to interview some of my own officers who were working in the Medway Towns Division in Kent. However, as their divisional commander and with the rank differential between us, it was likely that their answers would have been biased in significant ways. The answer was found through the work of Dr Susan Edwards of the Polytechnic of Central London, who replicated a series of structured interviews with police officers in order to elicit their approaches to marital violence. As her team had already carried out a similar research programme in the two London police divisions of Islington and Hounslow, it was possible to make a direct comparison between two groups of officers from different forces. In view of the fact that I held the rank of Divisional Chief Superintendent in the area where some of the research was to be carried out, it was clear that difficulties could arise if the police officers approached for interviews realized they could be identified and possibly held to account for their attitudes or replies. Suitable safeguards were built into the selection procedure so that the officers who were approached could be reassured that their identities would not become known to anyone outside Dr Edwards' team.

The structured interviews were run in December 1985 and January 1986. The 18 officers interviewed, all constables, had between $3\frac{1}{2}$ and 15 years service. Seven female officers took part in the interviews, with a range of $3\frac{1}{2}$ to 9 years service. Of these, 50 per cent were married. The 11 male officers in the sample had a service record of between 5 and 15 years. All of the male officers, bar one, identified themselves as married. One female

31

officer and one male officer failed to identify their length of service or marital status. All of the officers interviewed were post-probationers, i.e. they had completed more than 2 years service. In this respect, it was acknowledged that they were not a completely representative sample of all ranks and ages. However, they did represent a broad spread of service and experience from those on the operational side of the police, who would normally be expected to deal with marital violence during their day-to-day duty. They did not represent all ranks or specialist departments within the police service, such as the criminal investigation department, but one strength of the sample was that they had all actually had some dealings with marital violence. Their views were therefore formulated from operational experience, in addition to any other influences such as personal relationships or personal bias. When viewed against the greater sample taken in the two Metropolitan Police divisions by the same interview team, the results and answers obtained appeared to be similar.

A full analysis of the interviews is contained in Chapter 6.

Questionnaire for victims of marital violence

Most previous research on the subject of marital violence has explored the experiences of the victims and, in some cases, has exploded some of the myths surrounding the subject, e.g. that marital violence is exclusively working class, or that because the women stay in the marital home, they must enjoy the violence.

Most of this information was gathered for academic reasons, or by members of women's welfare organizations. By asking relevant questions, new areas of understanding could be uncovered. For example, some commentators are critical of the number of incidents of violence where prosecutions are later abandoned, often citing a lack of interest or sympathy by the police towards such incidents as the reason (Edwards, 1986; London Strategic Policy Unit, 1986).

As a means of exploring this area of the subject, a questionnaire was devised to test victims' involvement with the police and the legal system following incidents of marital violence. It was designed to try to get to the heart of the attitude of the victim towards the police response to their particular incident or incidents.

The first problem was identifying and finding victims; the second was finding the means to interview them. Identifying a reasonable sample of women 'victims' proved to be relatively simple, and despite problems concerning those who had returned to violent men, it was possible to trace and interview at least some women. Women police officers had access to several women's refuges where victims of violence, not previously known to the police, could often be found and who were willing to complete the questionnaire through an interviewer. Other sources of 'victims' were also found through local contacts, who, because of their excellent relationship and confidence in the policewomen's department, passed on information. Some of the questionnaires were run at the Canterbury Women's Aid Refuge, others at the Luton Refuge by their liaison officer, and still others at the Cardiff Refuge by South Wales women police officers.

When planning the sample, it was necessary to avoid the conscious selection of subjects, especially where they were residents of refuges. Individual women who had come to our notice outside the refuges tended to be selected simply because they came to our notice at a particular time. So far as the subjects resident in refuges were concerned, the governing factors were the availability of the interviewers, the availability of subjects at convenient times and their willingness to be interviewed. No attempt was made to select women for any particular reason, nor was any attempt made to achieve a spread of different backgrounds. They were a random sample of refuge residents at the time of the research.

There were both advantages and disadvantages in using policewomen to conduct the interviews. First and foremost, they were readily available as a valuable resource and it was possible to employ them on this research without any difficulties. Secondly, as police officers, they were in a privileged position in the community, able to gain access to information, as well as access to refuges, records and other services. They also gained trust and credibility very quickly. They readily responded to briefings on the questionnaires, having a great deal of previous background knowledge of the subject themselves, and they were trained in the taking of statements in a concise and factual manner – an advantage when trying to keep strictly to the questionnaire. It had to be acknowledged that because women police officers were being used to conduct the interviews and gather information, this may have built a measure of bias into the replies of some of the women concerned. However, this was generally unavoidable, especially where women living in the community were involved. It would have been virtually impossible to approach them by utilizing civilian interviewers, because of the question of access to such information and the additional expense which would have made the exercise impossible. The fact that police officers were conducting these inquiries, and that they had access to this confidential information, led directly to victims who would not have been discovered by other services and organizations. Therefore, it was possible to find some women who had never been in contact with social services departments, women's refuges or any other caring agency.

Despite the relative ease of identifying and having access to victims, there was the possibility of answers being biased because the interviewers were policewomen. On the whole, the interviewers reported a good rapport with their subjects, the majority of whom appeared to be at ease with their interviewers. Answering the questionnaires was often an ordeal for the women, however, because some were reliving extremely painful experiences, which they would rather have forgotten.

The final study used a sample of 38 women, which, although not on quite the same scale as that by Dobash and Dobash (1979) in Scotland, or Pagelow (1981) in the USA, was nevertheless sufficiently large to develop a meaningful statistical base, from which conclusions could be drawn. The analysis of this work is contained in Chapter 4.

Survey of policies of Chief Police Officers of England and Wales

It would be a mistake to believe that there is one common policing policy in the UK. Undoubtedly, in the last 25 years, there has been a more unified approach to police work in this country, but it is still a fact that policing priorities differ in each of the 43 police forces in England and Wales. The Home Office plays a part in drawing the attention of chief officers to new trends. It also recommends courses of action to them, but has no actual power to direct or coerce them if that advice is ignored, or not acted upon to the full.

There was a concern to examine those factors which influence the policies of chief officers and lead towards changes in their priorities. The question of *discretion* became a strong side issue during the course of the research. It required more attention than had at first been anticipated, for it became obvious that discretion was at the heart of the decision-making process as far as chief officers were concerned. On the other hand, operational police officers use their discretion whenever deciding whether to make an arrest for an alleged criminal offence.

In theory, at least, what happens in operational terms in a police area is the result of instructions promulgated by respective chief officers to the men and women under their command. The police service is a disciplined service, and the actions of all police officers are subject to sanctions if they breach the provisions of the Police Discipline Code. All policies and processes are set down in individual force instructions, which are the formal orders of the chief constable to his officers. In practice, therefore, there are 43 separate force instructions operating in England and Wales, each setting down the method by which individual matters will be dealt with. The concern was to try to compare and contrast individual force orders. In particular, the research pointed towards specific instructions for dealing with marital violence. Just as important, however, was the lack of such direction. I was also anxious to identify good working practices where they existed, something rarely found in examples of purely academic research.

Hanmer *et al.*'s (1989) experience of the reluctance of some forces to discuss their force policies was not unique among researchers, and previous experience with similar enquiries had shown that the number of completed questionnaires was often disappointing. Our first return was extremely encouraging, 37 of the 43 questionnaires being sent back completed. By sending out further reminders, a 100 per cent return was achieved, something which assisted the accuracy and relevance of the information contained in them. This result was also achieved 3 years later, when a second, identical questionnaire was completed.

The interest shown by a number of organizations and individuals in this subject, has demonstrated the concern that exists regarding the role of the police in marital violence and the expression of hope that changes will follow. This was summed up by an article in the *Daily Telegraph* (28 January 1987): 'The attitude of police forces to wife beaters is hardening. But too much is still left to chance. A nationwide policy is needed.'

4 — The victim's expectations and needs

There can be few people who would disagree that the most important person in the complicated web surrounding marital violence is the woman, unless children are involved. She is the primary victim and often the helpless – and sometimes hopeless – prisoner of years of physical and mental torture. As Pahl (1982: 339) comments:

> Most of the women had been physically assaulted over many years by the men with whom they lived, often since their first pregnancy or since the birth of their first child: 62 per cent said that the violence had gone on for three or more years. The injuries that they had suffered varied from cuts and bruises, through black eyes, broken arms, noses and ribs, to a ruptured spleen and a fractured skull.

These experiences are reproduced in the findings of many other researchers and commentators. For example, Dobash and Dobash (1979) found that many of the 109 women in their survey had been systematically beaten for several years before seeking refuge or assistance from some social agency, and an average of 11 incidents of violence were tolerated by the women in their survey before positive assistance was sought. Horley (1988) puts the number of assaults as high as 35. A *Woman Magazine* survey (February 1985) found that 14 per cent of its 800 women respondents had suffered serious injuries at the hands of their partners. In June 1987, *Woman Magazine* published the results of a second survey, this time with 7000 respondents. A random sample of 1000 was extracted, from which it emerged that 28 per cent had suffered violence at the hands of their husband or boyfriend. One woman respondent who had been subject to violence for some considerable time commented:

Last time my husband attacked me I couldn't walk for five days. I was unable to use my hand and bled for days from him kicking me in the stomach. In front of my terrified children, he threatened to put petrol through the letter box and set it alight. When I called the police they said, 'Get him to hit you again and then we will arrest him'.

The views of the victims on the quality of the overall service they had received from the police were clearly of great importance when considering the implications for future policy and practice in the police service. It was also important to discover exactly what the expectations of the women were, either when they called the police or the police attended in response to some other caller, such as a neighbour or friend. Did women want their partner arrested and prosecuted, or did they, as some people have suggested, merely want the police to stop the beating and to frighten the man off? Had the women ever initiated a complaint, only to withdraw support for a prosecution at a later date, as many police officers contended? Were the police as unhelpful as some commentators suggested? These questions were addressed by means of a questionnaire devised in the early stages of the research and completed by a number of women who acted as interviewers.

The questionnaire and the interviews

The questionnaire was divided into four parts. *Part 1* dealt with the woman, her background and previous history, including details of her children and her own nuclear family. It also included questions on whether her parents were violent, either to each other or to the children. This line of questioning was an attempt to address the notion of an inter-generational pathology of violence and learned patterns of behaviour, where it is suggested that some women learn violence as children and then see it as 'normal' in adult relationships. This hypothesis is contained in the work of Pizzey and Shapiro (1982) and Kemp and Kemp (1978).

Part 2 was concerned with the violent partner, his background and with gathering information similar to the questions asked of the woman.

Part 3 asked each woman about the violence used against her. This section was divided into two: the first and worst times her partner assaulted her. For ease of reference, the two sections were printed on different coloured paper – blue for the first and pink for the worst. (It was originally intended to include a third section on the last time the woman was assaulted, but this was eventually omitted because the complete questionnaire was becoming inordinately long and it was felt that the first and

Table 4.1 Interviewers and interviewees

Interviewer no.	*Location*	*Nos interviewed*
1	Medway Towns, Kent	17
2	Canterbury, Kent	8
3	Luton and Dunstable, Bedfordshire	4
4, 5+6	South Wales	9
Total		38

worst were probably the most important of the three occasions.) The section sought to explore both the incidents in their entirety – from the length of time the assault lasted, the reason(s) for the assault (if known), and whether the police were called and who called them – to the action the police took and what the victim did after the event.

Part 4 was a general section covering the woman's expectations of the police, and her reasons for taking certain actions, including the decision whether to support or withdraw a prosecution against her assailant.

A total of 38 women were interviewed during the course of the research, by 6 interviewers. The geographical locations and numbers of persons interviewed are shown in Table 4.1.

The women

The age range of the women interviewed was as follows:

20–30 years	13
31–40 years	17
41–50 years	8
Total	38

Six of the women had been an only child, whereas eight of them had come from quite large families with five or more children. The largest family consisted of 10 children. In the case of the women, there was no co-relation between size of family and violence towards any of the children, or between the parents. Only seven women in the survey had been personally subjected to violence by their parents and only eight had actually witnessed violence between their parents. There was no direct evidence, therefore, that the violence had been 'learned' prior to the actual violent relationship referred to in the interview, as in the Pizzey and Shapiro (1982) or Kemp and Kemp (1978) studies. These findings matched the results of Andrews'

(1987: 9) research, who found only 'a weak and statistically non-significant association between early violence in the family of origin and the risk of becoming involved in a later violent relationship'. All of the women, bar one, had children of their own and, in addition, five had stepchildren to care for.

By using information on employment, educational qualifications and housing, it was possible to estimate the socio-economic group (SEG) to which each woman belonged. The majority of those interviewed were in the lower SEGs, or could have been broadly described as 'working class'. However, the sample also included two graduates and some who could be described as 'professional women'. This reflected the findings of Dobash and Dobash (1979), that marital violence transcends social classes and boundaries and is not limited to any one particular class. It could have been anticipated that a large proportion of the women would have been drawn from the lower SEGs, in view of the fact that many of them had been interviewed in refuges, which often have a disproportionate number of women from the lower end of the social spectrum. The fact that some of the women had been part of large families was also shown to relate to social class and possibly to religious background, although this specific inform-ation was not sought.

The men

The age range of the partners of the women interviewed was as follows:

20–30 years	11
31–40 years	19
41–50 years	6
51–60 years	2
Total	38

In general, the men were slightly older than their partners, with one or two exceptions, but in most cases there was no more than 5 years difference between partners. It was interesting that 18 men, as opposed to 8 women, came from families where there were five or more children. It was also noted that 13 of the violent men, as opposed to 7 of the women, had themselves been subjected to violence by their parents, and that the majority of them came from larger family groups. Thirteen of the men, as opposed to eight of the women, were known to have been brought up in violent parental environments (although these were not all the same 13 men who had been beaten by their parents). The answers to questions relating to the men were clearly more unreliable than the answers to the same questions about the women. The women were answering for their partners' experiences and, in many cases, were not in a position to give a definitive reply. The socio-economic groupings of the men by and large matched those of the women with only a few exceptions.

There was no evidence to suggest that the breakdown in these relationships was caused by a short courtship, because 28 of the couples had known each other for at least a year before getting married or beginning living together. In one case, they had known each other for 8 years prior to getting married. It is interesting to note that 14 of the women had already been assaulted by their partners before getting married or cohabitating.

The first battering

The majority of the first assaults took place 1 year or more after the couples married or started living together ($n=26$), but the remaining 12 varied from periods of weeks to months. Pahl's (1982) findings, mentioned earlier, were reproduced in this study, and showed that many of the women had suffered beatings over a considerable period of time.

By using the definitions contained in the Offences Against the Person Act, 1861 (discussed more fully in Chapter 1), and applying them to the women's descriptions of the injuries, it was possible to indicate what criminal offences had been committed (if any). The majority of the injuries were cuts and bruises, but some were more serious and a few required extended treatment in hospital. Some could have been described as 'life-threatening' incidents. Two of the women in the sample miscarried as a result of an assault. Slight injuries, such as bruises or a black eye, were assessed as 'actual bodily harm', whereas the more serious injuries, such as broken ribs, scalding or wounds, were rated as 'grievous bodily harm' or wounding. The distribution of injuries sustained was as follows:

Grievous bodily harm	5
Actual bodily harm	26
No injuries	7
Total	38

Eleven of the women who received injuries felt that they should have received medical treatment, but in the event only eight actually did. One woman admitted that she had been too scared to seek medical attention; the other two did not give reasons.

The worst battering

The worst batterings, as might have been expected, produced more severe injuries than the first, and there was a shift from actual bodily harm offences to those amounting to grievous bodily harm or wounding. The breakdown of injuries was as follows:

Grievous bodily harm	15
Actual bodily harm	14
No injuries	4
No second time	5
Total	38

The classification of the injuries was once again arrived at by applying each woman's description of her condition following the beating to the definitions contained in the Offences Against the Person Act, 1861 (see Chapter 1). Without actually seeing the injuries, or having the advantage of medical opinion, it is difficult to categorize them accurately; however, the women's descriptions were sufficiently descriptive to arrive at some sort of classification. Thus, 'severe bruising' has been classified as 'actual bodily harm', as was the case with first batterings, although it is acknowledged that this could possibly have been grievous bodily harm or wounding, if the degree of injury had been severe enough.

The injuries sustained in the worst batterings varied from slight bruising to severe cases of fractures, stab wounds and burns, often leading to unconsciousness and hospitalization. Of the 23 women who believed that they needed to seek medical treatment, 3 felt that they were unable to do so for one reason or another. The term 'no second time' refers to those cases where the first battering was the *only* incident, because the relationship came to an end thereafter.

The time-scale over which the batterings lasted varied from 2 minutes, involving a short argument followed by the assault, to the longest battering, where the woman was kept a virtual prisoner in her home and subjected to repeated beatings for 12 days.

About half of the women who were involved in these incidents considered calling the police. Eventually, however, only nine actually did so. In another 9 cases, a third party called for assistance, usually a neighbour or relative. The alarming information to emerge is that the mental state of 13 of the women was such that they dared not consider calling the police for assistance, because they were in fear of their lives or were unable to get to a telephone. Of the remaining two women, one was on holiday at the time of the assault, and did not know how to contact the local police, and

Table 4.2 How women perceive the response of the police

	Helpful		Sympathetic		Supportive		Informative	
	First	Worst	First	Worst	First	Worst	First	Worst
Yes	2	13	1	13	1	6	2	6
No	2	7	3	8	3	7	3	4
No answer	2	6						

the second did not do so because she had had a bad experience of the police on the first occasion. Of the original 38 women in the sample, 5 were not included in the 'worst incident' data because they had terminated their relationships before a second incident took place.

Of those women who contacted the police, 13 did so by telephone, but 8 went to the police station either to seek assistance themselves or as a result of the police coming to their homes. One woman actually approached a police officer in the street. When asked about the actions/attitudes of the police officers who dealt with their cases, the responses were as shown in Table 4.2.

There were some mixed views expressed by the women interviewed, and not all the positive answers were unequivocal. For example, some women found the police helpful and sympathetic, but unsupportive and not at all informative. Others found them helpful and informative, but unsympathetic and unsupportive. One woman found the police unhelpful, unsympathetic, unsupportive, but informative. There were 26 positive reactions, set against 15 negative ones, but when one considers the seriousness of the injuries involved in these cases, which amounted to at least 29 cases of actual or grievous bodily harm, one would have hoped for a more positive response from the police officers concerned.

Reasons for the violence

The women offered a variety of reasons as to the cause of the violence used against them by their partners, in both the first and the worst battering episodes (see Table 4.3). It is worth comparing these results with the findings of Dobash and Dobash (1979:247), which are reproduced in Table 4.4.

It can be seen from both Tables 4.3 and 4.4 that sexual jealousy was the main reason given for the violence in both studies – 42.1 per cent in my study for the first battering, as opposed to 31 per cent in Dobash and

Table 4.3 Sources of conflict leading to violent episodes

Sources of conflict	First		Worst	
	n	%	n	%
Sexual jealousy	16	42	12	32
Expectations about domestic work	—	—	—	—
Money	4	11	5	13
Status problems	1	3	4	11
Relatives and friends	—	—	—	—
Drink	4	11	1	3
Children	2	5	3	8
Other	8	21	7	18
No reason	3	8	1	3
No second time			5	13
Total	38		38	

Note: Percentages are rounded to the nearest number.

Table 4.4 Sources of conflict leading to violent episodes

Sources of conflict	Violent episode							
	First		Worst		Last		Typical	
	n	%	n	%	n	%	n	%
Sexual jealousy	31	31	28	30	21	22	48	45
Expectations about domestic work	37	37	32	34	31	32	17	16
Money	7	7	12	13	11	11	18	17
Status problems	3	3	3	3	6	6	3	3
Sexual refusal	6	6	1	1	2	2	2	2
Wife's attempts to leave	5	5	7	7	15	15	0	0
Relatives and friends	3	3	1	1	2	2	4	4
Husband's drinking behaviour	1	1	1	1	2	2	7	6
Children	5	5	6	6	6	6	4	4
Other	2	2	4	4	2	2	3	3
Total	100	100	95	100	98	100	106	100

Source: Dobash and Dobash (1979).

Dobash; and 31.5 per cent in my study for the worst incident, compared with 30 per cent in Dobash and Dobash. Money was a slightly more important factor in my study (first: 10.5 per cent; worst: 13.1 per cent) than in that by Dobash and Dobash (first: 7 per cent; worst: 13 per cent).

Several reasons for conflict were often brought into play in one incident, so that a row which started over children sometimes developed into one concerned with money or sexual jealousy. The term 'other' covered a variety of reasons, ranging from drugs to one man who tried to force his pregnant wife into a life of prostitution!

Alcohol played a lesser role than might have been expected, having been cited as the principal cause of the *first* battering by four women, and as the cause of the *worst* battering by only one woman. It was mentioned as a secondary cause on six occasions in each of the first and worst incidents. It may have been a contributory factor in some of the other cases, but as the women were asked about the main reason for the argument, alcohol did not always figure in their replies.

Contact with the police after the first battering

Only 11 of the women actually considered calling the police following the first battering. In the event, four of them actually did. In a further three cases, the police were called by a neighbour, a friend and by a Women's Aid refuge. The women who did consider calling the police but failed to do so were either too frightened of what their partner would do, or were physically prevented from making the call. The majority did not consider calling the police and gave a variety of reasons, the main one of which was that it was the first time they had been assaulted and they were so surprised that calling the police did not occur to them. One woman had only been married that day and did not wish to appear foolish. These results are similar to those reported by Dobash and Dobash (1979), who found that victims rarely sought help or advice in the first instance and only looked for assistance after a number of violent incidents.

Of the women visited by the police, three felt that they were sympathetic and helpful, while one felt that they were not. Only three women answered the question 'Did the police do what you wanted them to?' Of these, two answered 'yes' and one answered 'no'. Other women contacted different third parties for assistance, not always with positive results. These varied from relatives and neighbours to professional people, such as doctors and social workers.

In four of the cases where the police were called, the man was arrested for a criminal offence. In two of these the women withdrew support for the prosecution at a later date. The other two cases went to the magistrates' court where they were disposed of. In the first case, where the woman had suffered actual bodily harm, the man was charged with a breach of the peace and conditionally discharged for 1 year. In the second, the assailant was charged with grievous bodily harm and fined £50, as well as being bound over to keep the peace for 1 year. It can be seen, therefore, that of 31 cases of either actual bodily harm or grievous bodily harm, only 2 resulted in criminal charges being brought before the courts, and one of these was not actually for causing injury to the woman. Binney *et al.* (1981) observed that in only 20 per cent of life-threatening cases was an arrest made; in cases where there was actual bodily harm, this fell to 15 per cent. Faragher's (1985) findings support these observations, and he noted that the police felt unable to help women in this situation because of their status as 'wife'.

In none of the incidents surveyed was there an injunction in force, but this was to have been expected, because this part of the questionnaire was only concerned with the first time these women were assaulted.

Police action

The response of the police officers with respect to the assailants was no better. Arrests were effected in only five cases, and in two of these the charges were not related to the injuries the women sustained, but were for breach of injunction and criminal damage, respectively. In one case, the assailant was reported for summons. Therefore, in 25 of the injury cases where criminal charges could properly have been brought, no criminal action was commenced.

Four injunctions were in force in the sample, three of which had powers of arrest attached to them. Three of the arrests which were made by the police were in those cases where injunctions with arrest were in force, although in only one case (involving no injury) was the man ever charged with breaching the injunction. The view of the Women's National Commission Report (1985) was that injunctions were only of limited value, even when a power of arrest was attached:

> ...it is virtually impossible for the police to assist in enforcing an injunction with no powers of arrest attached, and, probably through lack of specific training and lack of serious concern with domestic matters, police have often proved ill-informed about what to do, and sluggish to act, even when powers of arrest exist. (para. 108)

The powers of arrest attached to the injunctions seem to have had an effect in the cases under review, because all of the injunctions were upheld and actioned, even when there was no injury caused to the woman.

Response of the courts

Considering how serious some of the injuries were, the courts handed down relatively minor sentences to the offenders. The breach of injunction carried a verbal warning from the judge, the criminal damage case attracted the most serious sentence of 3 months imprisonment, and was followed by a fine of £200 for grievous bodily harm. The remaining cases were dispensed with lesser penalties.

The views of Pizzey and Shapiro (1982), Pahl (1982) and Binney *et al.* (1981) all focus on the reluctance of the police to take effective action which may be seen to offer protection to the victims of marital violence. Likewise, the ineffectiveness of the courts to show the disapproval of society for the pain and indignity suffered by the women, is also demonstrated.

The wishes of the victims

Of the 38 women in the study, only 3 actually stated that they wanted their assailants arrested. Most of the women wanted the police either to remove the man from the home or get them away from the man or the beating. Where the police took positive steps, the woman was always in accord with their actions and felt that they had fulfilled her expectations of them. When the police appeared unhelpful or unsupportive, they attracted the most negative comments.

In three of the cases, the victims suggested that it would have been helpful to have had a woman officer involved in the investigation, presumably because they felt that a woman would have been more sympathetic to their circumstances. In one American study (Kennedy and Homant, 1983: 391), 60 per cent of the victims interviewed said that they preferred to have at least one policewoman present, although 52 per cent said that they also wanted a male officer in attendance. Where some kind of family fight was involved, the majority of the women wanted the presence of two male officers.

In the worst battering incidents, police attended the family home on 17 out of the 19 occasions when they were called. Of these 17 incidents, women officers were present on 7 occasions. An analysis of the victims' reactions to the presence of women officers showed that they felt positively towards the police on four occasions (one of which was qualified), and negatively on three occasions (one of which was qualified). These results tend to follow the findings of Berg and Budnick (1986), who observed that women officers tended to adopt the attitudes and values of their male counterparts when dealing with a variety of policing problems, thus negating the assertion that women officers would be likely to adopt a more sympathetic line than a male officer. This is an interesting subject, but one this study did not have the time and opportunity to pursue more fully. However, it is a topic which deserves attention among British police forces, as most previous studies have been carried out in the USA.

Women's attitudes to the police

The women were asked whether their expectations of the police had been fulfilled. Ten of them replied unequivocally that they had, and a further five replied positively but with some reservation, or they added a comment. Fourteen women were quite certain that their expectations had not been fulfilled, and a further two replied negatively but with further qualification.

The unqualified 'yes' replies are self-explanatory, but the qualified ones included statements such as 'I didn't expect the police to do anything, so I wasn't surprised when they didn't.' Again, the unqualified 'no's' were obvious, but two women added riders: 'I was upset when they didn't come, but when they did, they were good' and 'I don't think the law gives enough protection to women in my position.' If these cases had merely involved shouting or assaults where no injury had actually been sustained by the women, then the 10 unequivocal 'yes' replies would have been seen as reasonable. But set against the background of the number of injuries sustained by these women, one would have expected a greater level of satisfaction with police action and fulfilment of their role.

When questioning the interviewees on the role the police played in their particular incidents of violence, it was of interest to note the influence that the police exerted over any decision to support a prosecution, compared with the influence of other parties, such as relations or friends.

Why women stay with violent men

The question 'Many people would probably like to ask you why you stayed with your husband as long as you did', evoked a variety of responses:

Nowhere to go	16
Because of the children	15
Because I loved him	10
He was OK otherwise	10
To help him through a problem (sorry for him)	8

Fear of consequences 6
Pride – not wanting
    people to know 3
Financial dependence 3

Some women specified more than one reason for not breaking up the relationship. For example, 'nowhere to go' and 'because of the children' were often linked, as were 'because I loved him' and 'to help him through a problem (sorry for him)'. In the case of the last two responses, the woman's loyalty for her partner often shone through the pain and indignity of it all, especially where she made a statement such as 'he was OK otherwise'.

Influences on prosecutions

Each woman was asked whether 'At any time after the assault did you feel that anyone tried to influence your decision to prosecute your partner?' Their replies were as follows:

No-one 22
Police 10
Relations 7
Friends 3
Solicitor 2
Doctor 1
Work colleagues 1
Women's Aid 1
Partner 1

The influence exerted did not always take the form of urging the victim to withdraw charges; in one or two cases, the police tried to persuade the woman to prosecute, as did some relatives. However, most of the influence exerted *was* of the negative kind, apparently in an attempt to persuade the woman to 'drop the charges' against her partner.

It is interesting that the influences, both positive and negative, did not always have an effect, and many of the women made a point of saying that they had made up their own minds. Among those women who did consider a prosecution, 24 did not withdraw support and 7 did.

The two reasons cited most frequently for withdrawing support were fear and to give reconciliation a chance.

Once again, the women felt the influence of the police to be negative and unsupportive, in that on eight occasions pressure of one kind or another was brought to bear for them to withdraw support for the prosecution.

Table 4.5 Effects of violence
on the behaviour of children

Effects	No.
Behavioural problems	13
Fear	8
Bed-wetting	5
No effect	11
No children	1
Total	38

Sandra Horley, writing in *Police Review*, appealed to police officers dealing with marital violence to act positively against the men who perpetrate such violence, even if the women are reluctant to help actively in the prosecution:

> Even when dealing with a hostile witness, I urge police officers to keep taking cases to court. It may be frustrating and unrewarding, but it will lay down a pattern of practice, which, in the end, will ensure that justice is seen to be done. (Horley (1988: 227)

The effect of the violent environment on children

The interviewees were asked whether they or their partner had been brought up in a violent parental environment. As mentioned earlier in this chapter, there was little evidence that marital violence had been learned from situations such as this, either by the violent man or the victim. What did emerge from the survey was the effect that living in a violent environment had on the children of the couples concerned. Of the women in this study, 26 identified changes of some kind in their children's behaviour, actions or attitudes as a result of the violence between the parents. Their children were often affected psychologically, leading to a fear of men or a particular man, to bed-wetting or other disturbed behaviours (see Table 4.5).

The term 'behavioural problems' covers individual forms of disturbance or behaviour, particular to a certain child or family, and encompasses terms such as 'withdrawn', 'poor performance or non-attendance at school', 'guilt', 'asthma', 'reluctance to marry', etc. Only one of the women had no children. The fact that two-thirds of the children suffered in some way because of the violence, is a question of some concern and one which deserves further serious consideration.

The questionnaires show unequivocally that most of the 38 women concerned in this study did not receive a very helpful or supportive service from either the police, or the law. In total, 60 criminal offences were committed during the course of the first and worst incidents, not to mention breaches of injunctions, and in only 4 of the 60 cases were charges brought for causing injury to the woman. The Metropolitan Police Report into Domestic Violence (1986: 37) reached the conclusion that the police could be criticized for:

1 A failure to provide victims with adequate protection and not making arrests in cases of serious assaults.
2 A lack of sympathy towards women and, in particular, abused women.
3 Responding in a purely statutory way.

This study supports these criticisms, and it was noted that a repeated pattern of inaction was found in the way police officers dealt with incidents of marital violence.

Other services and agencies also provided little help. The courts did not seem to view the injuries seriously and the highest penalty imposed was for criminal damage. In addition, it must also be said that very little help was forthcoming from any other quarter.

Undoubtedly, tremendous pressures, stresses and tensions are brought to bear on a couple going through the trauma of the breakdown of their marriage, and these clearly influence the logic of any given situation. One woman, asked to comment on the questionnaire and whether the questions had got to the heart of her situation, replied: 'It doesn't show how outside pressures such as parents, family and society forced me to stay on trying to make the marriage work.'

Positive help for the majority of these women was provided by Women's Aid refuges, and one has to wonder where some of these women would have ended up if it had not been for their help. Several of the women had been moved by Women's Aid from their home towns to another area for their own safety. During the time that the co-ordinator of the Canterbury Refuge was assisting in the completion of the questionnaires, one of the women in her refuge was murdered by her husband as she took her children to a nearby school. In another instance, one of the policewomen interviewers, commenting on the circumstances of the interview, said: 'The first time I called on this woman, she practically dragged me though the front door, near hysterical, stating that someone had got to help her.' There is no doubting the seriousness of the plight of these women, but at the time of their greatest need for assistance, very little help was forthcoming.

5 — Formulation and application of police policy

Possibly one of the most interesting questions raised in this study has been the way that official policy is, or is not, translated into practice. At the top end of the decision-making pyramid is the chief officer, be he the commissioner, as in the case of the Metropolitan and City of London forces, or the chief constable, as in other forces. It is he who sets down both the operational policy and the priorities which he expects the force to follow. At the base of the pyramid are operational police officers who are expected to translate that policy into practice and to follow the policy line set by their chief officer.

The police service is a disciplined service, that is, it is governed by a code of discipline, rather like the armed services. Any breach of this code of conduct carries certain sanctions set out in the police discipline regulations. The word 'discipline' comes from the same stem as the word 'disciple', which is defined as 'a follower or adherent of a leader of thought, conduct, etc' (*Concise Oxford Dictionary*). From this it can be inferred that a person in a disciplined organization is 'a follower' of the leader and bound to follow his policies and decisions.

The constitutional position of the chief constable is an interesting one in the British system. Although appointed by the police authority for a city or county, he is not their servant (*Fisher v Oldham Corporation*), nor is he an organ of local government.

The Royal Commission on the Police (1962) produced a report from which the Police Act, 1964, was later framed. It is this Act which forms the structure of the British police service as it exists today. The Royal Commission on the Police took evidence from many sources, one of which was the Association of Chief Police Officers, which described the constitutional position of the chief officer as follows:

51

because he holds the office of constable [he] therefore enjoys full protection from local control in carrying out his duties of law enforcement and in commanding his force for this purpose.

It went on to say that:

Quite clearly a police authority cannot direct a chief constable as to the manner in which he should carry out the enforcement of the law or the maintenance of 'The Queen's Peace', any more than they could direct any other constable on the exercise of his individual authority. (Royal Commission on the Police, 1962: 26)

The same point had previously been raised by Lord Chesham in the House of Lords in 1958 when, speaking on behalf of the government, he said, 'In the exercise of this responsibility he [the chief constable] is answerable to the law alone and not to any public authority' (Royal Commission on the Police, 1962: 26)

The role of the police authority is defined in the Police Act, 1964, as follows:

1 To secure the maintenance of an adequate and efficient police force for the area.
2 To appoint the chief constable (subject to the consent of the Secretary of State).
3 To determine the number of persons of each rank in that force.
4 To provide and maintain buildings, structures and premises.
5 To maintain vehicles, apparatus, clothing and other equipment required for police purposes.
6 To appoint deputy and assistant chief constables (Police Act, 1964, Sections 4 and 5).

Unlike the heads of the fire, ambulance and education services, the chief constable is not an officer of a council department as such, although appointed by one of its authorized bodies. However, the police authority will be seen to have considerable powers to provide, or possibly to withhold, certain resources or facilities.

The duties of a chief constable were also defined in the Royal Commission Report and were later embodied in the Police Act, 1964. In chapter IV of their report – that concerned with the purposes of the police and their constitutional position – the Commission cited Scottish law which prescribed these duties as:

to guard, patrol and watch so as –

i) to prevent the commission of offences against the law

ii) to preserve order, and
iii) to protect life and property.
(Royal Commission on the Police, 1962: 26)

The Commission acknowledge that:

> the policeman works in a changing society and there is nothing constant
> about the range and variety of police duties, just as there is nothing
> constant about the pattern of crime, the behaviour of criminals, the state
> of public order or, at deeper levels, the hidden trends in society that
> dispose men to crime, to civil and industrial unrest, or to political
> demonstration. The emphasis on particular duties varies from one
> generation to another.

The Commission recognized, therefore, the uniqueness of the chief
constable's position. It held that he should be free from undue political or
parochial influence, but answerable for his actions to the criminal and civil
codes of law. However, it also acknowledged the changing character of
policing and the responses necessary to deal with those changes. It is
implicit in the Royal Commission's analysis that the chief constable shall be
capable of recognizing, analysing and dealing with the demands that
society makes upon the police. Chief Constable Kenneth Oxford of
Merseyside referred to the police 'responding to changing times,' and also
to 'the fundamental changes which have influenced our society and which
have had an influence on almost all forms of human behaviour and
organisations' (Oxford, quoted in Benyon and Bourn, 1986: 61).

The constitutional position of the constable, as distinct from the chief
constable, was also identified and discussed by the Royal Commission. The
definitive case relating to the relationship of the police with the local
authority (*Fisher* v *Oldham Corporation*, 1930), contained in the *obita dictum*,
reference to another case, that of *Enever* v *The King*, 1906. In the case, Mr
Justice Griffiths commented as follows:

> Now, the powers of a constable, *qua* police officer, whether conferred by
> common law or statute law, are exercised by him by virtue of his office,
> and cannot be exercised on the responsibility of any person but
> himself. . . . A constable, therefore when acting as a peace officer, is not
> exercising a delegated authority but *an original authority*. (Royal
> Commission on the Police, 1962: para. 63; my emphasis)

The importance of the constitutional position of both the policy maker
(chief constable) and the operational officer who is charged with the
responsibility of both upholding the law as well as following his or her
chief constable's policies, is fundamental to the question of the arrest and

charging of violent men in domestic violence situations. Although the chief officer has the power and discretion to lay down the priorities and the general policies an officer must follow, there is no power which allows a chief officer to overcome the constable's 'original authority' to initiate prosecution. When the Women's National Commission (1985) recommended that 'officers should undertake arrest of persons perpetrating violence in the home, and should not use their own discretion', they were clearly unaware of the difficult legal position this would create. To take away the discretion of an officer when deciding whether to make an arrest or not, or some other legal process, would place him or her in a delicate and vulnerable legal position. All police officers, when they are acting as such, carry certain enhanced powers over and above ordinary citizens. However, under the civil law of this country, they may be held responsible for their actions if they exceed those powers, or act against the proper rights of an individual. As was discussed in Chapter 2, a police officer may be sued as an individual for any wrong he or she may have caused to another person, and to take away his or her judgement regarding arrests in cases of marital violence would create a legal minefield for police officers. The likely consequences would be that police officers would avoid dealing with marital violence wherever possible, exactly the opposite of what the Commission was trying to achieve.

Discretion and policy making in the police service

A generally accepted definition of 'discretion' is 'the liberty of deciding as one thinks fit, either absolutely, or within limits' (*Concise Oxford Dictionary*). Adler and Asquith (1979: 1). However, when considering the relationship between discretion and power in public office, adopted Davis' usage of the term 'discretion'. According to Davis (1971):

> A public official has discretion whenever the effective limits of his power leave him free to make a choice among many possible courses of action and inaction.

It may be argued that these two definitions of discretion are similar, and it is of interest to see how this process of discretion works within a policing context.

Scraton (1982: 6) comments on the different levels of discretion in the police service:

> At the level of operational practices, police officers use discretion in various ways. First, as the law does not cover every eventuality, and is sometimes even contradictory, police officers must use discretion in their

assessment of situations and enforce the law accordingly, i.e. they must decide whether a situation is 'likely' to lead to an affray or a breach of the peace. The use of discretion here is quite proper and necessary.

He goes on to identify discretion at the level of chief officer, which is brought into play when he is deciding on the policing priorities of his area. As an example, Scraton cites the clampdown on pornography ordered by Chief Constable James Anderton in Manchester in 1981, which was seen by some as a moral crusade, and as a necessary police operation by others. In other police areas, offences such as unlawful gaming or prostitution could be targeted in a similar manner if they were perceived either by the chief constable or his local commander to be a problem and to warrant the commitment of police resources. 'Discretion', Scraton (1982: 6) suggests,

> therefore not only operates at two fundamentally different levels – policies and practices – but also means different things. In terms of the law, police officers use discretion in its interpretation and its application. In terms of police organization they use their discretion in the ways they apply the force rules and their senior officers' commands. In terms of political controls chief officers operate a certain level of discretion in relation to elected representatives (the police authorities) and the government (the Home Secretary).

Discretion is a many-faceted concept and can function in several ways. For example, the policy of the Metropolitan Police regarding 'deferred decisions', relies on the discretion not to prosecute an alleged offender for marital violence, provided he remains out of trouble and does not repeat the offence in the next 3 months. Following the successful termination of this period, and provided he has not re-offended, a caution is administered. Although this policy is still in its infancy, the indications are that this use of discretionary powers may have a positive effect in the right type of case.

It is important to understand the role and function of police authorities in the running of police forces. The Royal Commission on the Police (1962) recognized the historical importance of locally elected representatives, as well as that of justices of the peace, who traditionally had been responsible for keeping the 'Queen's Peace'. The Police Act, 1964, set up police authorities in all of the forces (apart from the Metropolitan Police Force, which is a special case): they were to comprise two-thirds elected representatives from the area concerned, and one-third justices of the peace. The role of the police authority was defined in Sections 4 and 5 of the Act.

How then does discretion operate at these levels in relation to domestic violence? So far as the chief officer is concerned, police time and resources will only be committed if he perceives marital violence to be a serious enough problem. For this to come about, however, the problem has first to be identified. And here is the first of many difficulties. Edwards' (1986) work with two divisions of the Metropolitan Police Force indicated that there was considerable under-reporting by the victims of marital violence. Secondly, of those incidents reported, only a small proportion were actually recorded as crimes: 'The tip of the tip of an iceberg' as Edwards calls it. Even when they were recorded as crimes, the statistics did not actually record the fact that they were criminal injuries stemming from a matrimonial dispute. The matter was simply recorded as 'actual bodily harm' or 'wounding', as the case may have been. Therefore, there is often no permanent or cumulative recording of marital violence. Bourlet (1986) drew attention to the recommendations of both the Parliamentary Select Committee on Violence in Marriage (1975) and the Women's National Commission (1985), which indicated that the identification of violent crimes in marriage was essential to the proper understanding of the problem at both a local and national level.

In some forces, the identification of marital violence statistics has become possible on a local or force basis due to the acquisition of more sophisticated computer programs. In the area policed by the South Wales Constabulary, in one week in September 1986, 333 'domestic dispute' calls were received at the force's control room, and in the whole of both 1987 and 1988 over 20 000 similar calls were received. Not all of these calls, however, involved disputes between spouses or cohabitees, because in police terms 'domestic dispute' encompasses all domestic relationships, from husbands and wives to neighbours or family relations. However, computer technology is now available and more police forces are beginning to collect and analyse such data. Assuming that chief officers identify marital violence as a problem that warrants specific policies or action, positive advice or instructions will be laid down for the guidance of the force. Hitherto, much of that advice has been of a cautionary or negative character, as the early police instructions quoted in Chapter 2 illustrate.

Questionnaire on domestic violence policy

All 43 police forces in England and Wales are separate and autonomous. The structure of each force conforms to the 1964 Police Act. Each force is commanded by its own chief officer, who gives instructions as to the way in which specific incidents should be dealt with in the pattern of operational policing. These force instructions are framed in this way for two reasons:

1 In anticipation of complications being experienced when dealing with certain sets of circumstances or subjects.

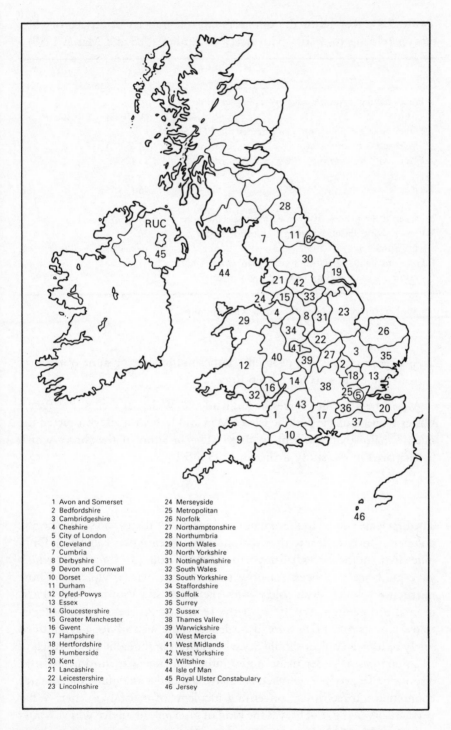

1 Avon and Somerset	24 Merseyside
2 Bedfordshire	25 Metropolitan
3 Cambridgeshire	26 Norfolk
4 Cheshire	27 Northamptonshire
5 City of London	28 Northumbria
6 Cleveland	29 North Wales
7 Cumbria	30 North Yorkshire
8 Derbyshire	31 Nottinghamshire
9 Devon and Cornwall	32 South Wales
10 Dorset	33 South Yorkshire
11 Durham	34 Staffordshire
12 Dyfed-Powys	35 Suffolk
13 Essex	36 Surrey
14 Gloucestershire	37 Sussex
15 Greater Manchester	38 Thames Valley
16 Gwent	39 Warwickshire
17 Hampshire	40 West Mercia
18 Hertfordshire	41 West Midlands
19 Humberside	42 West Yorkshire
20 Kent	43 Wiltshire
21 Lancashire	44 Isle of Man
22 Leicestershire	45 Royal Ulster Constabulary
23 Lincolnshire	46 Jersey

Figure 5.1 The geographical locations of the police forces involved in the study

Table 5.1 Results of the questionnaire on policies or advice of chief officers relating to marital violence (November 1985 and March 1989)

	1985	1989
1 Forces having a specific advisory policy or force order	9 (20%)	36 (78%)
Forces having a policy on action under the 1976 or 1978 acts (or equivalent)	24 (52%)	8 (17%)
Forces with no advisory policy or force order	13 (28%)	2 (4%)
Total	46 (100%)	46 (100%)
2 Forces in the process of formulating a specific policy	3 (7%)	—
3 Forces giving specific training to officers (post-probationer)	16 (35%)	26 (57%)
4 Forces maintaining statistics other than Home Office crime statistics relating to marital violence	10 (22%)	22 (48%)

$n = 46$. Percentages rounded to nearest whole number

2 As a result of previous problems, either in the force or some other area, from which lessons have been drawn.

All of the 43 police forces in England and Wales, as well as the Royal Ulster Constabulary, and the Isle of Man and Jersey forces, completed the questionnaire that was sent to them. The location of the forces which participated in the study is shown in Fig. 5.1.

Force orders

The first issue related to the extent to which police forces had set up specific policies or force orders to deal with marital violence (see Table 5.1). Only nine (16%) of the forces had a specific advisory policy or force order which gave guidance to officers on how to deal with marital violence. Those instructions which dealt solely with the Domestic Violence and Matrimonial Proceedings Act, 1976, or the Domestic Proceedings and Magistrates' Courts Act, 1978, were discarded, because such advice was confined solely to how an officer should act when arresting someone for a breach of an injunction or order made under either of these acts. In other words, disposing of a prisoner who had been arrested under an injunction, was not counted as a force order concerning incidents of marital violence. What was actually being sought was the kind of guidance or advice which would indicate that the chief constable and his senior officers were giving a positive lead in cases of marital violence. As an example, one set of instructions given to a northern police force was prefaced with these words:

Increasing concern is being shown about the question of violence in marriage or between persons cohabiting, particularly with regard to the problem of ensuring that, once a complaint is revealed, the offender is prevented from repeating the violence. This is a delicate area and it is accepted that any action taken by the police can only have a limited effect on the long term situation. The following instructions are, however, published for the guidance of officers attending family disputes etc.

This kind of advice was rarely given; indeed, 28 per cent of the forces actually had no force orders at all on domestic violence, and did not even give advice on what to do with prisoners arrested under injunctions.

The same force instructions went on to say:

In cases of serious wounding or grievous bodily harm, an arrest should generally be made. In cases of less serious injury, but where there is likelihood of a continuing breach of the peace, then the advisability of making an arrest should also be considered, provided there is evidence which would justify it. Whenever an arrest is made, a statement should be obtained from the complainant, unless this is physically impossible.

Though these were not the only force orders to contain such advice, there were not many that did.

The importance of a lead being given from the top emerged in two North American police initiatives – the first in Minneapolis and the second in London, Ontario. In each case, a strong policy statement from the chief of police set the standard for the police action that was to follow. Both of these initiatives followed pilot schemes which carefully compared various courses of police action in dealing with marital violence, before concluding that the arrest and charging of offenders produced the best results (i.e. lowest re-offending rates) (Sherman and Berk, 1984; Burris and Jaffe, 1984). Where no distinct policy has been formulated, or where no positive lead is given, it seems from the evidence gained from these studies that police officers will not identify the subject as problematical and any efforts are likely to be uncoordinated or fragmented. Although the circumstances in North America do not necessarily mirror those this side of the Atlantic, it would be interesting to see if the results could be reproduced here (see Fig. 5.2 for the results of the Minneapolis study).

It should be noted that the situation as depicted in the questionnaire returns (Table 5.1) was that found in November 1985. Since then, several

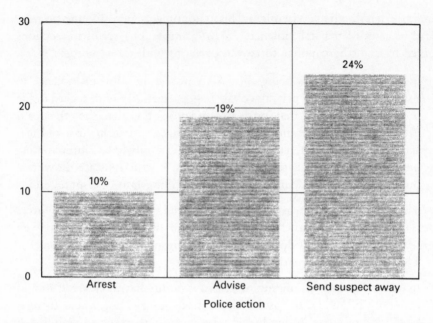

Figure 5.2 The results of the Minneapolis experiment (after Sherman and Berk, 1984)

forces have begun to formulate new policies and advice, and many influences have been brought to bear on the subject – magazine and newspaper articles have been written and television programmes produced. These have undoubtedly made an impact on the policies of chief officers, generally through more junior supervisory officers who were given the tasks of carrying out research and making recommendations. This culminated in a presentation to the autumn conference of the Association of Chief Police Officers in October 1988, by Sandra Horley of the Chiswick Rescue Centre, Woman Chief Inspector Maria Wallis of the Metropolitan Police, and myself. Following the conference, a number of forces either amended their existing policies or introduced new ones.

In view of the changing situation, a second identical questionnaire was despatched to the same police forces as in 1985. Once again a complete return was achieved and the results are displayed in Table 5.1.

Further training

The second issue studied was whether any further training on the subject of marital violence was given to officers after they had finished their initial 2 year probationary period. As probationers, officers are given instruction on a range of policing policies as part of a nationally agreed training package. Post-probationary training, however, is more discretionary, and therefore certain inferences can be drawn as to the importance placed upon a subject by whether it is included in the syllabuses of training courses undertaken by individual forces. In 1985, only 16 forces (35%) indicated that they gave specific advice/instruction on dealing with marital violence.

The range of courses on which advice instruction was given in the various forces was as follows:

- Sergeants' post-promotion,
- Sergeants' refresher,
- Detective training,
- Policewomen's specialist,
- Constables' refresher,
- Tutor constables',
- Community involvement,
- Warrants procedure.

By 1989, this figure had risen to 26 (57%), and several forces indicated that they were in the process of introducing this type of instruction.

Statistical records

Information was also collected regarding the extent to which forces maintained statistics other than those requested by the Home Office. It is well-known that the Home Office statistics do not differentiate between types of violence, and nor is the relationship of the victim requested from police forces or indicated in the published statistics. In 1985, 10 of the forces (22%) stated that they already maintained such information independently. One force in the north-west of England replied: 'Records are kept of all crimes of violence and sexual offences showing the relationship between the victim and the offender.' Another was actually able to give the following details:

Recorded Offences – 1984

Murder	10
S 18 Wounding	23
S 20 Assaults	53
S 47 Assaults	123
Total	209

The total includes one offence on a male person.

That is, of the 209 recorded incidents, 208 were assaults upon women by men.

These examples alone indicate that technically it is quite possible to gather and keep statistics that reflect the relationship between the victim and the assailant in violent crimes; in fact, some forces are actually doing this. Since the first questionnaire was completed, other forces have now acquired computer systems which are capable of gathering and storing this kind of information. In March 1989, 22 forces (48%) maintained information over and above that required by the Home Office.

From the evidence displayed above, it is apparent that there is no uniformity of policy or approach to marital violence within the police service in England and Wales, despite general advice and guidance from the Home Office, and the recommendations of the Parliamentary Select Committee and the Women's National Commission. The results emphasize the uniquely autonomous position that chief officers enjoy and their ability to prioritize with little or no reference to other persons or bodies. Although many more forces have now developed policies, are running courses that include marital violence, and are more easily able to identify the relationship between the assailant and the victim, the commitment is still not complete and there is no sign of a lasting improvement in the situation.

Discretion and good practice

Before finally assessing the value of the returns from the chief officers, it is first necessary to try to evaluate what may be judged as good working practice, as it applies to marital violence. Many commmentators and researchers have expressed their views as to what constitutes good practice in this field; however, to obtain an objective view, reference has to be made to the Select Committee Report on Violence in Marriage (1975) and the Women's National Commission Report (1985).

Having taken evidence from many different sources, the Select Committee made the following observation and recommendations on the section headed 'Police services':

> We understand the police reluctance to interfere in a citizen's domestic life and are not minded to recommend that policing practices change in any major respect. However, we do believe that assaults in the home are just as serious as assaults in other places and that citizens who call the police to their aid at a time when they are being assaulted are entitled to the full protection of the law. We recommend therefore that Chief Constables should review their policies about the police approach to domestic violence. Special instructions about this difficult and delicate

subject should be given to all new recruits, and regular written guidance should be issued by the Chief Constable in the form of advisory leaflets. It must be stressed that certainly where there is evidence of any injury the police should be ready to arrest the man there and then, subsequently to charge him and either keep him in custody until his appearance in court or, should this not be feasible, escort the woman and children to a Women's Aid refuge or other safe place. We deprecate the use of summonses in this situation, which leaves the man free until his court appearance. It may well be that, given this initial protection and if referred to a solicitor, the woman will prefer to pursue a civil remedy rather than a criminal one or there may be a reconciliation. Neither should be seen as proof that the initial police action was a mistake. Rather the reverse. This is not the kind of case where the conviction rate can be a justification of the initial action. We believe that effective police intervention in this area would do a great deal to reduce the problem of violence in this country and contribute to the prevention of a number of homicides. We further recommend that each police force keep statistics about incidents of domestic violence (See e.g. evidence p. 294) and that these statistics be recorded separately from other forms of violence in the National Statistics supplied by the Home Office. It is a well known fact that there is a shortage of police manpower. We cannot, however, accept this as a valid excuse for the police not being more effectively involved in dealing with the problems of marital violence. (Select Committee Report, 1975: para. 44)

In this one paragraph, the Select Committee encapsulated what it saw as the best working practices for that time. It is interesting to compare it with the questionnaires returned 10 years later. This was a thought echoed by the Women's National Commission Report (1985) in its recommendations on domestic violence. Best working practices in the fields of police training, procedures, information, liaison and referral were commented upon and changes were urged upon chief officers and the Home Office. It is clear from the results of the questionnaires that many police forces have still to implement the recommendations of the Parliamentary Select Committee and some have not yet moved towards the implementation of recommendations of the Women's National Commission, or Home Office Circular 69/1986. Here then is discretion at work. It is worth reflecting once more on Davis' (1971) definition of discretion, so far as it relates to public officials:

A public official has discretion whenever the effective limits of his power leave him free to make a choice among many possible courses of action and inaction.

The factors influencing change

Given these levels of discretion, what then prevents chief police officers from having absolute autonomy and resisting change at all costs? Would it not be possible for the chief constable to pull up his mental drawbridge and ignore the views of his police authority, the Home Office and the citizens he serves? The answer to this question, possibly, is 'Yes, but not for very long.' Not only is a chief officer accountable for his actions, but his policies are open to many influences.

It is important here to distinguish between 'accountability' (i.e. having to account for actions) and 'control' (i.e. having actions controlled or directed). A chief officer's operational decisions are not subject to control by any person, but they are accountable and subject to very strong pressures from a number of sources. According to Scraton (1982), pressure may be exerted on a chief officer's actions in a number of different ways as follows.

Public opinion

It is very difficult for a chief officer to ignore the influence of a campaign for change featured in the media (whether television, radio or the Press), and many a chief officer will be prepared hurriedly to review his policy if it is held up to question by the media. A number of examples of such action can be found in recent police history. The notorious Graef documentary film on rape in the Thames Valley Police area led a number of chief constables to review their policies and to adopt the recommendations of the Women's National Commission on Violence Against Women on how victims of rape should be dealt with (Women's National Commission, 1985). The decision by the Commissioner of Police for the Metropolis not to release the in-force working party report on domestic violence in 1986, attracted considerable comment in the media, and in fact was eventually leaked under the cloak of parliamentary privilege in a House of Commons debate and then reported freely in the Press shortly afterwards. This in turn led to considerable pressure being put on the Commissioner to make the report public and to review his policy on marital violence. It is often claimed that the police 'police by consent'. This is a claim that refers back in history to the origins of Peel's first police officers, who were recruited from 'the ordinary people'. As Reiner (1986: 7) puts it: '. . . by the 1950's policing by consent was achieved in Britain to the maximal degree it is ever attainable'.

In his keynote speech to members of the Police Superintendents' Association of England and Wales on 22 September 1987, the Home Secretary, Douglas Hurd, said:

The police service has already recognised the dangers of seeming to be too remote from the public it serves. It has shown itself ready to build bridges to the young and to the minority communities. It has shown an increasing willingness to listen to the views of the community, to take account of those views and to explain its actions.

Clearly a service that claims to serve the public must take note of its views. John Alderson, when he was the Chief Constable of Devon and Cornwall Police, became well known for consulting and liaising with communities and other services in an attempt to establish dialogue and tackle the problems of crime and social disorder. Alderson (1980a: 11) saw the process of influence as an inevitable compromise:

In a democracy, society evolves through competing pressures, which motivate the political processes. Police systems sometimes have to give gently to some pressures whilst at the same time standing firm against excesses.

Lord Scarman, who headed the Scarman Tribunal following the riots of the early 1980s, recommended that local consultative bodies be established to encourage consultation between the police and their communities. This feature was embodied in the Police and Criminal Evidence Act, 1984:

Arrangements shall be made in each police area for obtaining the views of people in that area about matters concerning policing of the area and for obtaining their cooperation with the police in preventing crime in the area. (Section 106)

With such levels of consultation, it is clear that any chief officer must be sensitive to the needs of his community and take heed of the views expressed therein. At what point the community starts to express concern about marital violence is a complicated issue. The fact that most marital violence occurs by definition within the family and in the privacy of the home, is one of the factors which makes it generally inconspicuous and unlikely to arouse public fervour. Pahl (1982) argues that the public/private dichotomy must be understood by anyone who wishes to help the victims of violence in the home, but its very anonymity makes it a cause in which both the state and the public are loathe to interfere. If the police are to be influenced to change their approach to the way in which they deal with marital violence, then public opinion has first to be changed. The Thames Valley rape programme, to which reference was made earlier, was one example where public opinion was seen to be mobilized in this way.

Political influences

Scraton (1982) argues that, although chief officers are theoretically immune from local political interference, they are nevertheless subjected to political constraints. At a national level, this in effect means the Home Secretary and the Home Office. At a local level, this means the police authority and, to a lesser extent, local Members of Parliament and councillors.

The Home Secretary has the political responsibility for policing in this country and the Home Office is the government department which administers that responsibility. The Home Secretary can influence chief constables' decisions in a variety of ways. First and foremost, he can introduce bills designed to change the laws that chief officers are bound to follow and administer (e.g. the law on the licensing of firearms), but more subtly the Home Office can give 'advice', which although they are not bound to follow, chief officers ignore at their peril. Linked to this last factor are Her Majesty's Inspectors of Constabulary, who are required by the Police Act, 1964, to inspect each police force annually and to certify that the force is 'efficient'. Dependent on this certification is the annual Police Grant from Central Treasury funds, amounting to 51 per cent (as at 1988) of the total expenditure on policing costs in the respective force (Police Act, 1964, Section 31). Annual force expenditures vary according to the size of the force concerned. For example, Dyfed Powis Police, with only 935 officers, had an expenditure of nearly £23 million in 1987–8; however, the Metropolitan Police, with 27 815 officers, had an expenditure of £875 million in the same financial year (Chartered Institute of Public Finance and Accountancy, 1987). The 51 per cent grant is no small consideration and no police authority could contemplate its loss. To date, the grant has never actually been withheld, but there have been cases where, to influence either police authority decisions or the actions of a chief officer, the threat of withholding the grant has been made. So far, a compromise has always been reached before the threat had to be carried out.

Advice is therefore promulgated by the Home Office via Home Office circulars, and this is generally noted and acted upon by chief officers. Home Office Circular 69/1986 gave advice to chief officers on the subject of 'domestic violence' in the following terms:

> The Home Secretary recognises the difficult and sensitive issues which may be raised for the family and for the police in cases of domestic violence, and that opportunities for intervention by the police may in some circumstances be restricted by the reluctance of victims to provide evidence. He believes, however, that there must be over-riding concern to ensure the safety of victims of domestic violence and to reduce the risk

of further violence, both to the spouse and to any children who may be present, after the departure of the police from the scene of any incident. Police officers will be aware of the powers of arrest which are provided in sections 24 and 25 of the Police and Criminal Evidence Act, 1984, and of section 80 of the 1984 Act, which provides for circumstances in which an accused person's spouse may be a competent and compellable witness. Chief Officers may also wish to consider the need to ensure their officers are in a position to provide assistance to victims of domestic violence by advising them how to contact victim support organisations and local authority agencies such as social work and housing departments which may be in a position to offer aid to victims. Such advice should be offered in private and might helpfully be contained in a leaflet which could be given to the victim. The Home Secretary recognises that the police had shown themselves sensitive to the needs of women who have been the victims of violent assault and have taken steps to ensure a sympathetic and helpful approach. He welcomes these initiatives.

Viewed against the background of the Police Act, 1964, it can be seen how diplomatically this circular is phrased. There is no hint of instruction or direction, and the text is couched in encouraging terms. However, it introduces one new element into the debate, i.e. that women should receive assistance in contacting support organizations and that this should be offered in private. It is also interesting to note the careful way in which the arrest question is introduced. There is no suggestion of policy or directive which could be misconstrued as interference; the latest powers are simply pointed out. Freeman (1987) is critical of this approach:

> This is a somewhat tame response by the Home Office. It leaves the interpretation of powers under the 1984 Act to the police and in no way directs a firmer response to domestic violence. It offers little sign of any changed policy or of any government initiative.

Freeman is right in stating that the circular does not signal any change of government policy, but to suggest that it is open to the Home Office to 'direct a firmer response' is to misunderstand the relationship between the Home Office and chief constables.

It is also apparent that this is only a brief piece of advice, because the text quoted above is the complete section that deals with 'domestic violence' and forms part of a circular drafted as a response to the recommendations of the Women's National Commission Report (1985). What is most noticeable is the lack of any reference to the reporting and recording of crimes of violence in marriage, an area in which the Home Office has a

67

direct interest as the department responsible for compiling the annual crime statistics for the UK.

One last point on this document is that it highlights one of the processes by which the attention of chief officers can be drawn to the findings and recommendations of a body such as the Women's National Commission, in the hope that new policies and initiatives will result. Several chief officers did respond to this circular. In South Wales, for example, an inter-departmental working party was set up to consider the implications of the circular, and it made a number of recommendations regarding changes to force policy, which have now been implemented.

Advice and assistance can also be given by HM Inspectors of Constabulary at any time during the year, not only during their annual inspection, when a more formal report is prepared on matters regarding force organization which require fine-tuning. The way in which a force deals with aspects of marital violence could form part of such advice. This would probably come about in response to a matter of public concern, or a media campaign which was beginning to gather momentum. HM Inspectors of Constabulary, who are invariably retired chief constables of considerable experience, would seek to advise chief officers on the case in point, but the content and timing are of great importance lest they be seen as political interference in the operational role of the chief officer.

The political influence of the police authority can be more oblique, but it can still be exercised without actually trying to interfere in operational matters. Police authorities have certain powers of discretion and action, and can make decisions for or against the provision of certain facilities or equipment. In 1986, for example, the police authority for the South Wales force, decided to fund three part-time female police surgeon posts for the examination of the victims of rape and serious sexual offences. At the same time, a policy decision was also taken to include victim examination and recovery suites in the designs of all future police stations. These discretionary responses were made to assist the chief constable's policy of implementing the recommendations of the Women's National Commission Report (1985). Without this assistance from the police authority, the chief constable would have found it more difficult to implement his policy. By way of contrast, during the mineworkers' dispute of 1984–5, several left-wing police authorities, sympathetic to the striking miners, tried to influence certain chief constables' options for taking action by refusing to provide equipment or facilities which would have been used by the police on picket lines, or in areas which brought them into conflict with striking miners.

Figure 5.3 'McBoot' (from *Police*, November 1987)

Personal factors

The influence of chief officers' personal career prospects and development on policy making is less obvious. Almost by definition, the person who attains the rank of chief constable must be a person of considerable drive, fortitude and ambition. He treads a difficult path, he is often in the public eye and is sometimes at the centre of considerable controversy. Any intemperate remark, lack of judgement or ill-conceived decision, could blight a promising career. Although it is in no way suggested that chief officers weigh every decision, action or policy against future career prospects, these considerations must, at some time, feature in the minds of such men, although to what extent depends upon the personal integrity and character of the officer in question. Chief constables can progress to command larger forces, to be commissioners, or to be inspectors of constabulary; indeed, the recognition of outstanding service can also be acknowledged through the honours list.

These are no small rewards for treading a diplomatic, compliant path. Anyone seeking to mount crusades or to develop policies which do not carry the tacit approbation of the Home Office or the public, may well find himself ploughing a lonely furrow.

It would be interesting to speculate on what influence activist, feminist organizations or academic research have had on the reformulation of police policy on marital violence. Much has been written on the lack of a police response to marital violence but, in effect, this has been tacitly ignored by the police. Reports such as that by the London Strategic Policy Unit (1986), are generally labelled by the police as politically motivated, after which they are generally dismissed. Some of this work has been supported by sound research and often carries sensible recommendations, but because it does not have the general support of the public, the media or the government, little progress is made.

It seems, therefore, that certain factors need to be present to bring about changes in force policy, or for some kind of review to take place. Scraton (1982) has identified some of these factors and there may well be others. Some areas of police work are value-laden or, at least, ideologically problematical. Wherever Davis' (1971) definition of 'discretion' applies, chief constables use that power to make value judgements which often do not accord with the views of all members of society. The perception which any chief officer has of the policing needs of his area will govern the disposition of police resources to deal with those needs. Those perceptions, however, are constantly being defined and redefined in the context of a changing society. This principle applies not only to police attitudes to marital violence, but also to many other aspects of policing. Crime, public order offences and traffic regulation are all policing problems which have to be assessed and re-valued in the same way, and they are all matters which constantly compete for attention. As Pahl (1985b) puts it:

> The debate, however, does not stop here. All who have written this book, and those who will read it, are themselves a part of the process by which social problems are defined and re-defined.

The next chapter will address how police policy is implemented once it has been formulated.

6 — Translating policy into practice

It is one thing for a chief officer to have a policy on marital violence, but it is another thing to translate that policy into practice. Chief constables are rarely personally involved in the supervision of such a policy, for that is not their function. However, they expect the policy to be carried out by the officers under their command, and supervised by those appointed to do so. The chief officer constructs or devises a policy (see Chapter 5), but it is the police constables who translate that policy into practice. Without the commitment of the officer to follow his or her chief constable's policy line, the policy might just as well have not been created.

In the last chapter, it was observed that not all chief constables actually have a policy or give advice to their officers on how to deal with marital violence. In circumstances such as these, therefore, it is necessary for officers to decide for themselves how to act when confronted with such a situation, within the framework of their knowledge of the law and their training in this area of police work. At first sight, many would find this approach attractive, in that it requires the officer to use his or her initiative and discretion regarding the question of arrest and prosecution. However, it can also have a negative effect from the woman's point of view, if the police officer fails to take positive action to resolve the situation. Pahl (1982) pointed out that some police officers experience conflict when deciding on the various courses of action open to them in 'domestic disputes'. Furthermore, there is often disparity in the way that wife assault is perceived by the police and by the women who have been assaulted.

The Parliamentary Select Committee on Violence in Marriage (1975) indicated that instruction and guidance should be given to police officers by chief constables on the subject of marital violence, and it spoke of the police being 'more effectively involved in dealing with the problems of marital violence'. This desire for increased police involvement, however, has to be viewed against the cardinal principle of 'original authority', i.e. the legal position of a police officer who initiates criminal action and which is identified by the Royal Commission on the Police (1962: para. 63). This principle holds that police constables have the vicarious liability for their own actions when deciding whether or not to arrest or prosecute an individual. An officer's discretion on whether or not to take action, therefore, plays an important part in the whole process, and it would take a fundamental change in British law to alter the situation.

Police perceptions of marital violence

Edwards (1986) set up a study in two Metropolitan Police divisions with the aim of:

> Examining the nature of the police response to domestic violence complaints and to isolate those factors relating to private attitudes, legal constraints, police priorities and policies, police training and police organisation which may have an impact on shaping this response.

The study was divided into two parts, the first of which involved an examination of (1) the station message books, in which all calls and callers are logged, (2) the incident report books, which are completed by individual police officers on the ground and in which all non-criminal incidents are recorded, and (3) the crime reporting system, in which all reported crimes are recorded. The second part of the study involved structured interviews with police officers whose operational responsibilities ranged across the whole spectrum of uniformed duties in the Medway Towns.

A total of 18 police officers took part in the Kent survey, 7 of whom were women and 11 of whom were men. Of the women officers, three were married, compared with nine of the men; two of the men and one woman officer failed to identify their marital status. The women officers were both younger and less experienced than their male colleagues. However, this was to be expected, because women officers tend to leave the service much earlier than men (see Table 6.1).

The interviews conformed to a predetermined checklist, so that all points were covered in the interview, although not always necessarily in the same order. The aim of each interview was to examine the role of discretion and influences internal to the police organization, police priorities, practice and assessment procedures, together with extraneous influences, such as the criminal justice system and personal attitudes. The

Table 6.1   Officers involved in the Kent survey

	Women (n = 7)	Men (n = 11)
Marital status		
Married	3	9
Single	3	0
No information	1	2
Length of service		
Under 10 years	6	3
10 years +	0	5
No information	1	3

interviews attempted to examine some of the problems faced by police officers when handling cases of marital violence, and to look more closely at the impact of individual officer's discretion on styles of policing and law enforcement practices.

In order to preserve anonymity, the Kent officers were chosen by a woman police sergeant, with no reference to the author or anyone else. There was no conscious selection procedure, except that the officers concerned should have had some experience of dealing with marital violence at some time in the recent past. The study sample could easily have been replicated in any other police force, because most uniformed police officers are called upon to deal with marital violence within their first 2 years of service, and on average have to deal with one or two cases per month, depending on their area of duty. Edwards was able to secure the cooperation of their officers who participated in this study, because anonymity was guaranteed.

Several key questions were explored: How did the officers rate the importance of marital violence calls in the context of contemporary policing? What were the officers' views about violence against women in general? The interviewers then moved on to examine whether or not these various views about violence against women had an impact on what action the officers actually took in such cases. Initially, the interviewers asked factual questions about police powers. They then asked the officers to describe the kinds of situations appropriate for arrest and subsequent prosecution.

Reiner (1985: 95) writes:

Domestic disputes are a common sort of call regarded as 'rubbish' by many police officers: With domestic disputes, the husband and wife

Table 6.2 How the police perceive their role in domestic disputes/violence

	No. who accept role			No. who do not accept role		
	Daily work	Mediators (piggy-in-the-middle)	Frustrating	Should not be involved	Piggy-in-the-middle	Waste of time
London (n = 44)	20	10	6	3	2	3
Kent (n = 18)	10	1	4	1	—	2

going hammer and tongs, you've got to separate them, calm them down before you go, you're not doing a policeman's job, you're doing a socialist's' [*sic*].

The much publicized Policy Studies Institute research on policing in London (1983: 314–15), similarly found that there was a certain amount of ambiguity regarding the perception of the police in relation to marital violence. Most officers had a negative attitude towards marital violence, often feeling that they should not become involved. Table 6.2 shows that although most officers accepted domestic violence as part of their job, there was also a certain amount of reluctance, frustration and ambiguity. On the other hand, some officers, usually those with first-hand experience, have a sense of urgency in relation to 'domestics'. As one put it:

> Society in general tends to knock the arse out of domestics, saying 'it's only another bloody domestic'. Then again they say 'it's only a shoplifter', but it's still a theft. Then again a domestic can become a murder as I know only too well (Kent officer no. 10)

On the whole, this kind of police work was not popular, and tended to be met with a resounding 'Oh no, not another domestic.' Reluctantly, most officers accepted that it was part of police work, but some of them felt that they never produced clear-cut results.

Young officers, in particular, felt uneasy about marital disputes. Their age and relative inexperience left them vulnerable and some of them felt that they lacked credibility, which gave rise to feelings of extreme discomfort. The Working Party on Police Probationer Training (1971) found that similar views were held by probationers at the beginning of their service. Most felt that their youth and inexperience often left them ill-equipped to deal with certain situations. However, the older officers

Figure 6.1 The scene of a domestic murder

interviewed by Edwards often felt frustrated when dealing with marital disputes. As one said:

> You get a piggy-in-the-middle feeling at times, you get let in but none of the parties are pleased to see you. . . . When we got to the address, they did not want us in. The woman had cuts on her arm . . . the man present was trying to bandage her up. They more or less told us to clear off, in fact they said, 'fuck off' (Metropolitan officer no. 13)

Some of the officers in the Kent study felt that their training had been limited and the majority of them would have liked to have had more. Others, however, felt that the best form of training came from practical experience in the field. One officer suggested that a greater knowledge of human awareness skills would help in this area.

Welsh Women's Aid (1987), in their *Annual Report 1986/87*, welcomed the recognition of mutual training needs following the All Wales Conference at Llandrindod Wells in November 1986. They spoke of 'reciprocal training', and suggested that Women's Aid had a role to play in sensitizing the police to the needs of women.

Enforcing the criminal law

As Chatterton (1981: 6) commented in the *Report of the Royal Commission on Criminal Procedure*:

> One of the most extensively documented facts about police work is that the police under-enforce certain laws and jealously protect the discretion which that implies.

The use of discretion in arresting an offender for breach of an injunction or for committing a criminal offence was influenced, according to the officers interviewed, by the seriousness of the injuries (objective) and the preparedness of the complainant to prosecute. The assumption that women are likely to withdraw charges, resulted in the emergence of four clear policing strategies when dealing with such cases (see Table 6.3):

- non-arrest;
- deferral of police action, i.e. 'cooling off';
- recourse to civil remedies;
- other measures, e.g. breach of the peace.

Some officers were reluctant to make an arrest because, in their experience, women did tend to withdraw their charges at a later date. Note the following comments:

Table 6.3 Effect of withdrawing charges on styles of policing

	Effect on police response			Other measures used		Not committed	No effect
	No arrest or prosecution	Delayed action	Recourse to civil remedies	Breach of the peace	Criminal damage		
London ($n=44$)	15	6	8	4	1	6	4
Kent ($n=18$)	7	2	1	2	—	2	4

There's a lot of work and you take statements, make a pocket book entry, nick someone, then there's the worry of everything being tickety boo for court, that takes about 16 hours, only for the husband or wife to say, 'thanks but no thanks'. You think all that bleedin' 'ard work is going out the window. (Metropolitan officer no. 13)

As a rule don't [arrest] because it could turn them both against the police the next day. (Metropolitan officer no. 7)

[I would arrest . . .] Very, very rarely, we don't just deal with domestics as such, if the wife has been hit and got a black eye she's full of it you know. Take him away, but invariably the next day she withdraws her statement. (Kent officer no. 1)

It depends when we think it was necessary or when it would serve a purpose, or if that is what the victim wanted; but combined with this we'd throw in oceans of discretion. The majority don't need arresting because it's not the answer. (Kent officer no. 5)

If one of the parties wouldn't calm down, if there's nothing you can do, do it that way. If there's a serious injury and allegations are made then you arrest. (Kent officer no. 6)

As a rule I don't. I've never arrested anyone for a domestic. If it spilled out on the street, or there was some danger to another party, I would arrest for a breach of the peace. But as a rule I don't because it could turn them both against the police and the next day they're 'lovey dovey' and we're the ones that caused the problem. Even if there was an injury, or an assault offence, I think it still wise to leave it for a while to let it calm down. Nine times out of ten, the other party doesn't want to know anyway. (Kent officer No. 7)

Cooling off

Officers tended to operate their own 'cooling off' period. This was especially apparent in one of the two London divisions investigated. In Kent, 54 per cent of the officers interviewed felt that a 'cooling off' period would be helpful to them in dealing with this problem. In some cases, they related this to social workers being called to give counselling to couples who were having a domestic dispute. Asked if a 'cooling off' period would be useful, one Kent officer replied:

I like that, under breach of peace I've nicked people but it's not strictly kosher. Lawfully if nicked, they should go to court next morning, but that means if you get nicked on Friday night you have to spend the whole weekend in the cell to go up on Monday. What happens if they tend to get nicked, is we keep them over night, let them sober up, have a quick word with the wife or the other party, it's all sorted out, smoothed over and then we release, but that's nowhere near the book. (Kent officer no. 13)

Other measures used

Frequently, when there is sufficient evidence to arrest for assault, officers arrest for a breach of the peace. Of the Kent officers, 38 per cent felt that carrying out an arrest for a breach of the peace was the most suitable means of dealing with such situations. Although not the only time it is used, it is often seen as a way of dealing with the offence without requiring the victim's compliance. Some officers linked making an arrest for a breach of the peace with the retraction of charges by victims at a later date. About 50 per cent of officers stated that the possible retraction of charges influenced the way that they dealt with marital violence.

Only 28 per cent of the Kent officers believed that they used discretion when exercising a power of arrest in this kind of case. This was rather surprising, in view of the degree to which discretion appears to be involved in cases of marital violence.

Enforcing civil law

In response to a question about the value of civil injunctions in preventing marital violence or assisting the police to deal with it, only 27 out of 44 London officers replied. Of these, 20 (74 per cent) thought they were 'a waste of time', 6 thought they were generally useful, and 1 felt they were of no use, even with an arrest clause. In the Kent study, 11 out of 18 officers (73 per cent) shared the view that injunctions without arrest were a waste of time and 4 thought they were generally useful, or effective.

In the majority of cases, police officers thought that injunctions were not effective in granting women protection from marital violence, and where there were breaches, the power of arrest was seldom enforced. Where the courts had granted injunctions with or without a power of arrest, both created problems for policing. First, officers were unanimous in stressing that injunctions without a power of arrest were 'useless', a 'waste of time' and 'not worth the paper they are written on'. Officers saw such injunctions as no more than a caution or a 'ticking off' of the offender – they felt that their powers were limited. Injunctions granted with a power of arrest, however, gave them the authority to arrest if they saw fit. In practice, however, few of the officers involved in the Kent side of the study said they would actually arrest men where injunctions had been breached.

Where men had returned to the matrimonial home, the women were often blamed for inviting them back, rather than the men being blamed for returning or accepting the invitation. The officers felt that it was up to the women to uphold the injunctions, although in fact the injunctions were served against the men concerned. Where women were considered to have allowed their men to return, for whatever reason, the officers felt that they had then forfeited their right to protection when the man became violent. One male officer remarked:

> From my experience, a lot of women have actually spoiled it for the rest. They get an injunction and then when the injunction is granted they invite the man back in. I mean I was called to a disturbance the other day. He is there on a Sunday. He said, 'I took her out for meal on Friday', and she says, 'OK you can come back for the weekend.' A lot of them actually use this and then when they've had enough of them they say, 'Out' and invoke the injunction. (Metropolitan officer)

The attitude to injunctions amply illustrates the complexity surrounding marital violence from a police point of view. Injunctions are granted by a civil court – either county or high court – where only the two parties concerned are represented. The police are not represented at the hearing and, indeed, are often not even aware of the existence of the injunction before being called to the marital home. There is no doubting the seriousness of breaching injunctions, but that seriousness is not always perceived by police officers attending such incidents.

'Rubbish' or social work

Much of the time that is spent on cases of marital violence, is taken up advising women of other courses of action. Police advice tends to be poor, in that police officers lack the necessary advisory and counselling skills, and the relevant information is not always available due to the poor relationship between the police and social service departments and other relevant agencies, such as Women's Aid. Edwards (1986) comments:

> In the Kent area officers had a particularly good relationship with the local Women's Aid refuge. Because of the effects of certain officers, police referred women to the hostel and were sympathetic to the work of the organisation. Similarly, officers at Hounslow had a negligible awareness of Women's Aid, simply because a refuge did not exist in their

area. By contrast, in Holloway, whilst at the time of researching, two refuges were in existence in the area, relationships were not only non-existent, they were hostile.

In some circumstances, the relationship between the police and other agencies is important, in view of the number of women who turn to them for support, but there is disagreement over a number of issues. The relationship between the police and the social services in Kent was described by Edwards as 'fair' (i.e. mediocre) and in Hounslow as 'not good'. In Holloway, however, the police were reluctant to use the social services at all in cases of violence or child sexual abuse, because of what they saw as a reluctance on the part of social workers to cooperate.

When the police officers in the survey were questioned about cooperation with other agencies, the range of bodies mentioned, included social services, Women's Aid, National Association of Victim Support Schemes, Citizen's Advice Bureaux and Marriage Guidance. The social services and Women's Aid were mentioned most frequently in both studies, whereas Marriage Guidance was mentioned only once. This reflected the experiences that officers had with other agencies regarding cases of marital violence. In Kent, relations with both the social services and Women's Aid were judged by the police to be better than they were in London.

In the Kent research, an attempt was made to ascertain how long officers tended to spend at domestic disputes. This varied between 'a few minutes' and 'a couple of hours'. The amount of time spent at the scene was usually influenced by the pressure of other work, the attitudes of officers to 'domestics' and the attitudes of the parties involved to the police presence.

The policing priorities at the scene of the dispute were seen as:

Protecting all concerned from harm	5
Protecting children from harm	5
Separating the parties	5
Quelling a breach of the peace	2
(One officer failed to respond)	

To this end, of those questioned, the majority identified the need to split up the parties involved, obtain the story and then try to establish the cause. They then usually suggested that the couple seek counselling or advice in order to attempt a reconciliation.

Officers used their own experience of life and marriage when proffering advice, which may indicate why the younger officers felt so inadequate. They were at pains to adopt a neutral position between the parties involved. A few of the officers interviewed found the experience irksome and a waste of time because they felt they were dealing with 'inadequate people'. In general, this stance seems to have been struck to avoid the principal question of whether a criminal offence had been committed. It implied that they were assuming that their own norms and values were appropriate for dealing with marital violence, rather than the application of the criminal law.

When asked if violence against women is ever justified, 80 per cent of those who replied in the Kent study felt that it could never be. The remainder said they thought that it could only be justified 'in self-defence' or 'under extreme provocation'.

Stead (1972) states:

> The British policeman or woman has, since the time of Peel's first professional police force in 1829, always been drawn from ordinary working-class people. This has been seen as a strength of the British policing system, because, not only are they drawn from that group, but they also live and work in that same community, in order that he/she should know and understand its needs.

However, in the case of some officers, the fact that they are drawn from a society where prejudice and bias abound, is a weakness, because they enter the police service imbued with the same prejudices and biases as the rest. Indeed, it would not be surprising for some police officers to hold the same views as those men they have to deal with. The *Woman Magazine* survey (February 1985) discovered that many of the wives who wrote to complain of marital violence were married to men in uniformed employment, among whom were a number of police officers. In this study, three of the women involved were married to police officers, a fact that had influenced them when deciding whether or not to call the police to deal with a violent incident. This could well have had an influence on the neutral stance some Kent officers adopted when dealing with such incidents.

What emerges from this study is that police officers often have a perception of marital violence which reflects a feeling of uncertainty. To enter the privacy of someone's home and intervene between two adult human beings who have been locked in an intimate and possibly loving relationship, seems to some to be unnecessary. Where it is obvious that both parties are capable of dealing with the situation by seeking legal advice, for example, police officers become frustrated when they are called to that same address many times over, only to have their advice ignored yet again. Therefore, it can be seen that the police view of 'domestics' does not always match that of the victims of marital violence (see Chapter 4), or some of the other agencies and organizations concerned. Some officers do not make the connection between criminal acts and acts of violence in the home, and they use their legal discretion to further the distinction between the two.

What appears to be essential in order to satisfy the sense of injustice so often felt by victims and their champions, is a fair and impartial discharge of the law so far as it affects everyone. Or, as Welsh Women's Aid (1987: 14) comments:

> Our main legal issue is why is violence when it occurs in the home not treated as a crime in society? We are concerned that existing legislation is not used to its full extent by courts and that this shows collusion with male violence.

These structured questionnaires certainly show that police officers are concerned about the welfare of women, but feel frustrated and uncertain when intervening in the home. This frustration is compounded when, following many inquiries, some of the women withdraw the charges against their partners. This frustration can be seen in such comments as: 'This is not a matter for the police, but should be dealt with by social services.' Many police officers, therefore, feel that marital violence should be dealt with by some other agency other than the police. It is important for police officers to receive further training and to develop closer ties with groups such as Women's Aid and victim support schemes, something which has begun in some parts of the country. These kinds of policies, which have been tried in Minneapolis and London, Ontario, will be discussed in the next chapter.

7 — Implications for the future

Marital violence exists in every country in the world. In a report to the Commonwealth Secretariat, Connors (1987: 1) indicated that marital violence was to be found in all of the 66 Commonwealth countries covered by the report:

> North or South, East or West, in rich countries or in poor ones, women are beginning to recognise that their many societies share one element in common: a frighteningly high proportion of violence directed against women, in the home, in the street, in the workplace. It is a violence that has been largely invisible, under-reported, unrecorded and often, tacitly ignored.

Despite this indictment, not all countries deal with marital violence in the same way. However, in the last few years, the authorities in a number of countries have taken vigorous action to deal more positively with this complex subject. In Minneapolis and London, Ontario, policies have been framed around a philosophy that persons who commit marital violence should be treated in the same way as they would be if the offence was committed in a public place. That is, they should be arrested. Canada has also increased the penalties for all crimes of violence, and advice has been given to the police in most provinces that they must prosecute in all cases of domestic assault, even when the victim would prefer not to lay charges. In New South Wales, provisions were introduced in 1982 and 1983 which have clarified the powers of the police to enter and remain in premises where an officer has reasonable grounds to believe that domestic violence has recently been, is being, or is likely to be committed, if the officer is invited to do so by a person who apparently lives in the premises, whether or not that person is an adult. New South Wales also took the unprecedented step of issuing certain warrants by telephone, where an officer was denied entry into premises indicated above (Connors, 1987: 19).

In this country, the subject of marital violence throws up an interaction between victim, the police and the law, which, when combined in this way, make up the model of what may be termed the 'British system'. This system of dealing with matrimonial violence is certainly reproduced in many other countries in the world, not necessarily by design, but often by default. What has become apparent, as a result of initiatives in the USA, Canada and Australia, is that there are other ways of approaching marital violence, which give a greater measure of protection to the victims, without the consequential overloading of the criminal justice system.

Several elements of the 'British system' have been examined during this study: police policy and its formulation; the translation of policy into practice, and the role that discretion plays in initiating prosecution; the victim's expectations of the police and her wishes in relation to prosecution. This study has considered the way that marital violence is regarded in both the criminal and civil courts in the UK, leading to the granting of injunctions, as well as the sentences imposed on men who commit criminal assaults against their partners.

Police policy in the 'British system'

During this study, the way in which the police deal with marital violence in England and Wales has been seen to come in for criticism from a number of sources. Police policy and practice has been based upon a philosophy of non-intervention, similar to that advocated in the Liverpool Police instructions of 1926, which, it will be recalled, cautioned police from interfering:

> ...especially between husband and wife, you will find that both will turn on you. (Liverpool City Police instructions, 1926 edition)

This philosophy was still having an impact on police policy in 1975, for when giving evidence to the Parliamentary Select Committee, the representative of the Association of Chief Police Officers endorsed the previously cautious approach of the police and spoke of their role as being a 'negative one' when dealing with 'persons bound in marriage' (House of Commons Select Committee on Violence in Marriage, 1975).

In Chapter 5, it was noted that only 9 of the 46 police forces canvassed had a specific policy or gave advice to their police officers on how to deal with marital violence. The fact that in many forces specific instructions on dealing with marital violence were not promulgated, does not necessarily mean that the subject was totally neglected. It is apparent in marital violence incidents that criminal offences of actual or grievous bodily harm are often involved. It may well be that other instructions were to be found in the force orders specifically covering these offences, and the attendant matrimonial circumstances may not have been seen as worthy of a special instruction. In other words, criminal assaults were adequately covered, but not in the section dealing with domestic violence or disturbances.

What is apparent from the study of initiatives in other countries, however, is that a strong policy statement from the chief officer, or other authority, is an essential precursor to the building of a positive operational policy, if that policy is to stand any chance of working. In January 1986, for example, the Chairman of the Ontario Police Commission, Shaun MacGrath, drew the attention of all of the police chiefs in the province, to the deep concern felt by the Solicitor General for Ontario over the consequences of 'domestic violence', and he stated that he himself shared in this concern. He drew attention to the encouraging results of an experiment in London, Ontario, where the police laid charges in all cases 'where reasonable and probable grounds exist'. He went on:

> I would, therefore, ask you to make your officers aware of these findings and to encourage them to continue to fully investigate these incidents when reported and to lay charges where facts and circumstances warrant. (MacGrath, 1986)

The results of this exhortation are not as yet recorded, but those from the London, Ontario pilot scheme, according to Jaffe *et al.* (1986), resulted in a significant decrease in the number of charges being withdrawn or dismissed, '. . . contrary to the common myth that victims would be less co-operative'.

In the other well-reported North American experiment in Minneapolis, a similar initiative showed that police intervention – which involved the arrest of the batterer – was approximately twice as effective in reducing victim–reported repeated violence during a 6-month follow-up, than the alternatives of the police offering advice or separating the couple for a short period of time. This initiative was also preceded by a supportive statement from James K. Stewart, Director of the National Institute of Justice, who commented:

> The answer, as this report documents, appears to be that the police should use arrests quite frequently in typical domestic violence cases if they want to reduce assaults. (Sherman and Berk, 1984).

It would be interesting to investigate the effects of a specific policy on the patterns of marital violence in the nine British police forces which had a policy on this subject, and to see whether this had made any impact on the problem. It would also be of interest to compare those results with police forces which had a similar problem, but had no set policy or advice.

The conclusion drawn from this study, however, is that a positive statement from the chief officer on the status of criminal assault in marital violence is necessary, as well as written advice on how such incidents should be handled. This study shows that without such a lead, reinforced by supervisory officers, constables may well adopt a negative approach to offences which have been committed and finalize the matter by giving advice, rather than by arresting the assailant. This conclusion accords with the views of the Parliamentary Select Committee on Violence in Marriage (1975: para. 44):

> However, we do believe that assaults in the home are just as serious as assaults in other places and that citizens who call the police to their aid at a time when they are being assaulted are entitled to the full protection of the law. We recommend therefore that Chief Constables should review their policies about the police approach to domestic violence. Special instructions about this difficult and delicate subject should be given to all new recruits, and regular written guidance should be issued by the Chief Constable in the form of advisory leaflets.

The means for bringing about such changes in force policy were discussed in Chapter 5. If the means can be found to influence public opinion, so that it is socially unacceptable to beat one's partner, then a change in policy will be forthcoming. A parallel can be drawn with drink and driving offences. Whereas it was once regarded simply as unlucky if a person was convicted of driving over the limit, since 1987, due to a change in public opinion, it has gradually become regarded as socially irresponsible. The drink–related accident figures for Christmas 1987 showed a reduction for the first time in several years, indicating that the message was getting through (Department of Transport, 1987).

Policing marital violence at the 'sharp end'

It is clear from the research among police officers in London and Kent that marital disputes, or 'domestics', are regarded as a frustrating and uncertain area of police work, and where there are rarely any clear-cut solutions. It is apparent from the replies of operational police officers who described themselves as being at 'the sharp end' of policing, that many of them felt let down by the victims, who sometimes withdrew their support for a criminal prosecution, or that they attracted undue criticism for what they saw as their role as mediators. As indicated earlier in this chapter, the approach in London, Ontario suggests that the idea that women withdraw support for prosecutions is a myth.

Edwards' (1986) conclusion is that many police officers feel that domestic violence should not be a part of their work at all. Any situation of this kind is simply seen as a complete waste of time. Another view that was held by some officers, was that it did nothing to assist them when applying for another post or for promotion. This view seems to ignore the fact that the police are charged with protecting life and property within the community, as well as 'prosecuting offenders against the peace'. Both these elements are strongly represented in cases of marital violence:

> We have already described the case where the police ignored a solicitor's letter asking them to arrest the man who was attacking her client. He murdered her later that day.

> In Southall a woman called the police the day before she died. They were unable to find any evidence that her husband had hit her. The next day she was found hanged. Her sister said later that she had endured eight years of misery ever since marrying her husband. (London Strategic Policy Unit, 1986: 36)

There are dozens of anecdotes to match these incidents, and in this study of 38 women, a total of 60 criminal assaults were revealed to have occurred. It leads to the conclusion that this is 'real' police work, no matter how awkward or frustrating the circumstances may be.

Discretion and the initiation of action

The Women's National Commission (WNC) recognized how discretion operated in this area of police work and recommended as follows:

> Senior officers should be concerned to ensure that, where Force Instructions require this, officers should undertake arrest of persons perpetrating violence in the home, and should not use their own discretion. (Women's National Commission, 1985: recommendation 18(iv))

Although it is apparent from this study that a reduction in discretion requires a fundamental change in the law, the same result could be achieved if chief officers followed the North American system and laid down a strong policy, such as is contained in the Minneapolis and London, Ontario statements, or, indeed, the WNC's recommendation, save for the part dealing with discretion. If such a policy statement were to be made, officers would be guilty of a disciplinary offence by ignoring criminal injuries such as those described by the women in this study. Some would argue that such a situation exists at the present time and that police officers' actions are already influenced in this way. However, we should not lose sight of the historical position of the British police service in its cautious approach, as contained in both the ACPO response to the Select Committee (1975) and the Liverpool Police Instructions of 1926. In the final analysis, it is the question of police attitudes, leading to an under-prosecution of criminal offences, which is the crux of the matter. The attitude expressed by one police officer, highlighted in Chapter 6, that, 'As a rule I don't [arrest] . . . . I've never arrested anyone for a domestic', must be resisted, both by chief officers and by supervisory officers who need to see that such a policy is implemented.

Injunctions were not liked by the police officers interviewed, although it was interesting to note that in all instances where there was a power of arrest attached to the injunction, the arrest clause was actually invoked. Police officers spoke of injunctions without arrest 'not being worth the paper they were written on'. In some respects, this may have been true, but there may have been certain advantages for the women if they had taken their partners back to court in the event of a breach. It is interesting to note that the UK has some of the most sophisticated legislation based on the injunction in the whole of the Commonwealth. According to Connors (1987), the British system suffers from the fact that it is encompassed in three acts of Parliament, namely:

- The Matrimonial Homes Act, 1983;
- The Domestic Violence and Matrimonial Proceedings Act, 1976; and
- The Domestic Proceedings and Magistrates' Courts Act, 1978.

The first act only applies to a woman who is married and who wishes to obtain exclusive use of the matrimonial home. The second act can apply whether she is married or not, and if she wishes to stop her partner molesting her. The third act provides parallel remedies to the second act, but only in the magistrates' courts, and then only for married victims. The weakness in the system is that it does not provide cover for all potential victims. Where couples are not married and are not living together, injunctions are difficult to obtain under this legislation. The net result of the British system, according to Connors (1987), is that it may often be avoided, because it is complicated and not always understood by the victims, or indeed, their lawyers. Although they were often thought to be worthless by some police officers, injunctions were seen to have some value when it came to enforcement. It appears that injunctions with arrest clauses are much more likely to be positively actioned by the police than those without them.

One of the contentious areas of marital violence that the police officers commented upon, was the reluctance of some victims to assist in a prosecution or their withdrawal of their co-operation at a later date. Several such instances came to light during this study, and others were revealed by Edwards and her colleagues. However, some of the victims revealed that the police often put pressure of one sort or another on them not to prosecute. Although it is fair to say that the police did sometimes put pressure on victims to support a prosecution, this pressure was typically found to be of a negative kind.

Edwards contends that Section 80(4) of the Police and Criminal Evidence Act, 1984, makes prosecution by the police easier in cases of marital violence. The section provides that:

> In any proceedings, the wife or husband of the accused shall be compellable to give evidence for the prosecution, or on behalf of any person jointly charged with the accused if, and only if, the offence charged involves an assault on, or injury or threat of injury to the wife or husband of the accused, or a person who was at the material time under the age of sixteen. (Edwards, 1986)

Although the Act makes it possible for a wife to be both 'competent and compellable' to give evidence in a criminal assault charge against her husband, Edwards does not take fully into account the impact of the wife's situation on the decision to prosecute. It is very difficult to fly in the face of a plea to discontinue a prosecution when this is presented on the grounds of reconciliation, or fear of the victim's husband. The police appreciate only too well the strength of feeling and the passions that are generated in these cases, and they are often moved to support a request for withdrawal when it is the last attempt to get the parties together.

On the other hand, it has been argued that if the police were to mount a prosecution, even in the face of a lack of cooperation from the victim, then powerful messages would be sent out to society at large. First, women would feel that the police would use the law to its full effect to protect them. Secondly, violent men in society would realize that marital violence is not acceptable and that they will be prosecuted in the same way as if they had committed a criminal assault in the public domain. Thirdly, society as a whole would see that the police intended to pursue rigorously such prosecutions and that such acts were against the interest of all of its members, not just the couple involved. Like drinking and driving, such acts must gather the contempt and distaste of society. As Connors (1987: 56) states:

Seldom is the perpetrator of violence made accountable for his behaviour. Where men are contracted by professionals, their denials and rationalisations are too readily accepted. If violent men are not made to take responsibility for their actions we, to all intents and purposes, condone their behaviour.

What must not be overlooked is that prosecutions are no longer taken before the courts by the police, but since 1 October 1986, when the Crown Prosecution Service came into being, they have been handled by that independent body. The decision whether to pursue a prosecution or discontinue it, is now their decision.

The expectations of the victims of marital violence must be appreciated more fully if the police are to improve the public perception of the way in which they deal with domestic disputes. Some commentators suggest that this ought to be a part of police training. However, I recognize that these matters are only of value if they can be put to use in operational circumstances. If the impression prevails that the police are not interested and feel the victim's call is a waste of time, the service they give will continue to be criticized and undervalued.

In Chapter 2, the Home Office lesson notes on domestic disputes were examined, and they advise as follows:

> ... there is usually no criminal offence involved and although the dispute may be an isolated occasion, it is common for some disputes to occur regularly over a long period. Police Objectives: – The objective of police attendance at the scene of a domestic dispute is to restore the peace. (Home Office, 1986a)

This study showed that criminal offences were involved in a large number of the incidents examined, and therefore either it is not representative of cases of marital violence or the lesson notes were misleading. The second point to be made is in relation to the stated objective of the police 'to restore the peace'. There is no mention of treating injuries, advising a woman about the existence of a refuge or ensuring her future safety, and advice is not given as to whether the officer should arrest the aggressor or not. All that is suggested is that the police should restore calm.

In this study, some officers expressed feelings of discomfort when dealing with 'domestic disputes', and said they were ill-equipped to deal with some of the situations in which they found themselves. The Working Party on Police Probationer Training (1971) shared this view and drew attention to the way in which a young police constable is advised and instructed in the early days of his or her service. The content matter of the initial recruit training programme is examined and approved by both the Personnel and Training Committee of the Association of Chief Police Officers, as well as by the Police Training Council, which comprises members of the three staff associations of the police service, as well as members of police authorities and the Home Office. Course time is already given on how to handle 'domestic disputes', but for a greater amount of time to be devoted to this subject or for there to be a change of content, there needs to be a change in national policy. The passage quoted above represents the prevailing policy of minimum involvement and disengagement. This once again underlines the need for a policy of positive action in such cases.

Training has been a key issue in achieving change in other parts of the Commonwealth, especially in Canada and Australia. As Connors (1987: 39) puts it:

> Certainly, police training must encompass specific training on domestic violence. This must be given to all police personnel rather than specialised units; very often resources make it impossible for special units to be generally available throughout a country. The response of the officer at desk level to an abused woman is critical; police must be made aware of the human and social side of their role, rather than focussing strictly on law enforcement. This may have important implications for recruitment as well as training. The steps towards police training which have been taken in other parts of the Commonwealth, for example, in Canada and New South Wales, should be monitored and considered.

The specialized units to which Connors refers have appeared in a number of police forces in England and Wales, mainly as a result of the Women's National Commission Report (1985). This took notice of Roger Graef's much-publicized *Police* programme featuring the Thames Valley Police in 1982, which showed an allegation of rape being handled in a very unsympathetic manner by male police officers. The Sex Equality Act, 1976, led to a total integration of women officers in the police service and, in turn, to the demise of their specialist duties relating to women and children. The Thames Valley episode exposed certain deficiencies and a lack of sensitivity in the way that women could be dealt with at a time when they were at their most vulnerable. Smaller, highly professional units have now begun to appear in some forces, in order to provide the service once again. The danger, as Connors so rightly points out, is that specialist units are not the complete answer, because the point of first contact with the woman is often so vital. 'The officer at desk level', as she describes it, needs to have the knowledge and training to deal with marital violence, because specialist units are not always readily available to deal with incidents in their early stages. Some officers in the Kent section of this study recognized two needs in the training field: some spoke of a need for 'human awareness skills', which may be interpreted as Connors' reference to 'the human and social side of their role'; and others simply referred to 'additional training'. It was interesting also that some felt there was no substitute for experience in the field to equip them for dealing with marital violence. The problem with this approach is that the first incident dealt with could be a life-threatening incident, and the victim in such a case cannot afford the luxury of waiting for the officer(s) to gain experience at her expense.

A fact that is not always known to the police is that women who work in womens' refuges also experience feelings of great frustration when one of their clients returns to their violent partner, and this is compounded when they go back several times. This emerged at the conference at Llandrindod Wells in November 1986, attended by police officers and volunteers from Welsh Women's Aid, where the opportunity was taken to share information and experiences regarding marital violence (Welsh Office, 1987).

Expectations and wishes of the victims

In Chapter 4, an analysis of the questionnaires dealing with the experiences, expectations and wishes of the victims of marital violence was undertaken. It was sometimes difficult to reconcile the attitudes of the police officers in the Kent study with the expectations the women had of the police. What most women wanted was to be believed, to be taken seriously and to be helped by stopping the violent man from continuing the violence. Not all of the women wanted the police to arrest and prosecute the offenders, but where this happened, there was full support for the police action. In fact, whenever the police took positive action, or adopted a sympathetic attitude, this met with the approval of the woman concerned. What most women seemed to find frustrating was a negative approach – that the police either felt that they could do nothing or that the women were wasting their time. Many police officers failed to recognize these frustrations and thought their role was either to restore the peace (as per the Home Office initial training notes), or to commence a prosecution. A greater awareness of the needs and expectations of victims on the part of the police seemed to be called for, and one would hope to see this come about through the exchange of information at training sessions, where women's groups could also share their experiences.

The police need to appreciate such factors as the repetitive nature of marital violence, and that the first occasion on which they are called to the marital home is unlikely to be the first occasion that the victim has been assaulted. Dobash and Dobash (1979) found that women had on average been assaulted 11 times before they eventually called the police, but Horley (1988) suggests that as many as 35 incidents may take place before help is sought.

Police officers should also receive counselling to resist making value or moral judgements, based upon role expectations and the differences between men and women, such as failing to deliver meals on time or clean the house. These should not be seen as excuses for violent episodes. The victims do not generally accept them as warranting the beating, and neither should the police. By observing these wishes, police officers will avoid the kind of critical observations levelled by Pahl (1978), Dobash *et al.* (1985) and Binney *et al.* (1981), all of whom reported that the police response was often unhelpful to the victim. Pahl (1982) discovered that those women who found the police to be helpful, were usually those who had learned about a refuge from them, had been taken to it in a police car or given overnight accommodation at the police station. She especially found that the police were described as 'unhelpful' when they seemed reluctant to become involved or intervene.

Home Office Circular 69/1986, reproduced in full in Chapter 5, suggested aspects of good working practice on marital violence. If the recommendations contained in it had been adopted by chief constables and embodied into force policies, then a tremendous step forward would have been taken. Several of these aspects were embodied in the report of the Working Party into Domestic Violence (1986), commissioned by the Metropolitan Police. It concluded that:

> the primary response of the police must continue to be that of prevention and an appropriate response. This is best achieved by:
>
> 1) prosecuting the offender;
> 2) giving practical assistance where required; and
> 3) offering accurate advice.

When compared with the Home Office Initial Training Notes (1986a), which merely advocate restoring the peace and advise that there is usually no criminal offence involved, it will be seen tthat the Metropolitan Working Party recommendations supplement the current advice given at training establishments and go a long way to meeting the expectations and needs of victims.

Police systems and statistics

Without exception, every book, study, article and critique which seeks to analyse the extent or incidence of marital violence comes up against a lack of hard statistics. This situation is by no means unique to the UK, for it is common to most countries. MacLeod (1980: 9) comments on the lack of official statistics in Canada:

The best information available at the present time on the victims of spouse abuse is found in the writings of academics and professionals who are analyzing data obtained from residents of shelters.

In 1975, the Select Committee on Violence in Marriage drew attention to the paucity of statistical information that was available on which to base any conclusions regarding trends in marital violence. Ten years later, the Women's National Commission (1985) repeated the same observation: in 1989, the situation has still not changed. If the problem of marital violence is to be fully understood and monitored, accurate statistics must be made available. If the geographic and demographic spread of marital violence is to be known, and proper financial and manpower resources allocated to deal with it, then information must be forthcoming. The means to gather information on the relationship between victim and aggressor is there – it just needs the political will to implement the decision that it will be kept. This would have advantages, not only for monitoring marital violence, but for assessing many other areas of criminal assaults.

In Chapter 5, it was seen that a number of police forces commented that they had the ability to gather statistical information on domestic disturbances and relate it specifically to marital violence. The Metropolitan Police Working Party Report (1986: 45) commented:

With the introduction of Computer Aided Dispatch (CAD) there perhaps has never been a better opportunity to gain the necessary statistics, for effective monitoring of domestic disputes.

Clearly, such electronic information gathering of statistics would be a great advantage in counting the number of cases of marital violence, especially in the absence of official Home Office statistics. Such systems have a further advantage, in that addresses where domestic disputes regularly occur could be flagged on the computer as a warning to officers attending the incident: it should not be overlooked that nearly 10 per cent of the injuries sustained by South Wales police officers between 1987 and 1989 resulted from domestic disputes. It is hoped that the provision of this type of command and control system will spread and continue, and be supported by research and development protects at both the national and local levels. In addition, the existence of injunctions affecting specific persons and addresses could also be retained on file for immediate reference should further calls be received. This also received the support of The Women's National Commission Report (1985).

In examining the nature and extent of marital violence in Chapter 1, it became apparent that incidents of violence are both under-reported and under-recorded. Edwards (1986) talks of 'the tip of the tip of an iceberg' in relation to the recorded incidents, and one can only speculate on their real level. Connors (1987: 12) is certain that the actual extent of marital violence will never be fully quantified:

> For reasons which include shame and humiliation, a victim is unprepared to complain about her situation. Even if the abuse becomes obvious to a third party outside the family, the victim will often explain it away, in terms to allay suspicion.

The only way in which the victim of violence can be encouraged to break out of this situation is to send strong messages to her that she will find a sympathetic hearing and supportive regime awaiting her if, and when, she decides to go to the police. Many of the victims dealt with in the course of this study have commented on the great relief they experienced on entering a women's refuge, simply because they were among women who had suffered the same experience and knew how they felt. It is clear that the police will have to work hard to alter the public's perception of their attitude to marital violence. This view was supported by the Metropolitan Police Working Party (1986: 31), which reported, under the heading of 'Public perception', that:

> The generally held view of the police response to domestic violence is that it is inadequate. It has been claimed that the police do not take domestic violence seriously enough, neither in their immediate response to a violent situation, nor in their attitude towards subsequent prosecution of violent offenders.

The black radical feminist singer Tracy Chapman included the following song – which indicates her strong feelings towards police inactivity – on her 1987 album entitled simply *Tracy Chapman*:

Behind the Wall
Last night I heard the screaming
Loud voices behind the wall
Another sleepless night for me
It won't do no good to call
The police
Always come late
If they come at all

And when they arrive
They say they can't interfere
With domestic affairs
Between a man and his wife
And as they walk out the door
The tears well up in her eyes

Last night I heard the screaming
Then a silence that chilled my soul
I prayed that I was dreaming
When I saw the ambulance in the road

And the policeman said
'I'm here to keep the peace
Will the crowd disperse
I think we could all use some sleep'.

The initiative must not end with the creation of a supportive regime, however, but must also be extended to include the proper recording and collating of crimes as they become known to the police. In her study of two Metropolitan divisions, Edwards found that a number of reported criminal assaults were not recorded if the women subsequently withdrew their support for a prosecution. This is clearly wrong, because the lack of support for a prosecution does not mean that the incident never took place, and there are other ways of writing-off crimes such as this without totally expunging the record.

Implications for practice

This study has succeeded in highlighting a number of points of concern, to society as well as to the police service. Although it did not set out to identify why marital violence occurs, it became clear as the study went on that much violence stems from the role expectations which are at the heart of intimate relationships between men and women. Without making value judgements as to the justice of such expectations, a man is perceived by many members of society as the breadwinner, master of the house and the driving force in a relationship, whereas a woman tends to be seen as the homemaker, mother, carer and as an adjunct or supporter of the husband. The ideologies which surround the popular concept of a companionate marriage, are worked and reworked by novels, newspapers and magazines, and women are portrayed in a subordinate role, with very few individual rights apart from those which attach to the husband or male partner. The worst aspects of a woman's position in a male-dominated society are portrayed in the tabloid newspapers, with their page three models and cartoon strips like *Andy Capp*. These concepts have a marked influence on the attitude taken by society to domestic situations. In recent legal history, it was considered acceptable practice to chastise children and wives, and there is the memory of the British judge who once pronounced that it was permissible to chastise one's wife provided a stick no thicker than a man's thumb was used (*Blackstone's Commentary on the Laws of England*, 1765).

Role expectations often reach crisis proportions when other factors, such as drink or jealousy, are added to the marital equation. The *Woman Magazine* survey showed that some police officers' wives are themselves subjected to violence and, furthermore, that some officers feel that the violence is partially or wholly justified, because the women have not fulfilled their domestic role. What emerges from such a study, is the need for a strong policy lead and adequate supervision of the outcome of police involvement. It has been suggested that supervisory officers should become involved in cases of marital violence where more than two calls from the same address are received. Supervisory officers could be sensitized to the needs of victims, the correct procedures to be adopted, and the way in which other agencies should become involved.

Attitudes and approaches of the police

The final implication, linked closely with the other two, is one of attitudes and approaches to the problem, both at chief constable level, where the initial policy decision is made, as well as out in the community, where the problems are dealt with. Evidence from the North American and Australian studies shows that other initiatives and models can work, provided there is the will at the top, reinforced by middle ranking supervisors. There are two real options: to do nothing more than is being done at present and to allow the existing unsatisfactory system to prevail, or to take a more positive stance against marital violence and transmit strong signals into the community that this kind of behaviour is not acceptable and will not be tolerated in a civilized society. The means are there to achieve this goal, and it would not be difficult to initiate and monitor such a policy.

8 — The way forward

One of the main objectives of this study was to explore the means by which the system of policing marital violence can be altered and improved. The police service has always reacted swiftly to counteract criticisms of its shortcomings. This has been epitomized in the wake of several notable cases which have led to an exposure of policing methods. In cases such as the Yorkshire Ripper Inquiry, the Cleveland Child Abuse Inquiry and the Hillsborough Football Stadium tragedy, the police service has acted quickly to identify its shortcomings and then correct them. Action to 'close the stable door' is generally very rapid, if often somewhat overdue.

In order to improve the service provided by the police and other agencies to the victims of marital violence, it is considered essential to learn from the lessons that emerged during the 4 years of this research. One question posed to officers who participated in the Kent section of the inquiry, asked them what they thought might improve the way police deal with marital violence. The following are some of their suggestions:

1 Police officers should be trained in human awareness skills and be able to recognize other peoples' perceptions of them (two officers).
2 There should be many more refuges available to women (one officer).
3 An overwhelming view prevailed that there was a need for much closer cooperation with the other services and agencies (10 officers), especially the social services department who, it was felt, should consider setting up a 24-hour service aimed at dealing with marital violence as it occurred (five officers).
4 Additional training would be advantageous, but it was felt that only experience in the field could really teach officers the most effective method of dealing with such incidents (five officers).

The need for training

Many suggestions for training have been identified during the course of this study, some of which have been recommended by the various official committees and bodies which have reported on this subject, others from informed writers and commentators who perceive the need for the police to develop their knowledge and skills, and some from within the police service itself. A synopsis of the recommendations is as follows:

Special instruction about this difficult and delicate subject should be given to all recruits. (Select Committee on Violence in Marriage, 1976: para. 44)

All basic police training for both uniform and CID should include insight into the nature and potential of domestic violence. (Women's National Commission, 1985)

Police Training should be modified to encompass specific training on domestic violence. (Connors, 1987)

During initial recruit training and during in-service training, the police force should instruct its officers that wife assault is a crime and they should follow a consistent procedure in every case. (Montgomery and Bell, 1986: 58)

Training should include:
• How to assist a woman attacked in the home.
• Awareness of non-physical and non-apparent physical injuries.
• Awareness of immigration legislation.
• Police officers and judges to undergo training on racism and sexism and impact of legal system on women.
• Information about Women's Aid and other agencies.
(London Strategic Police Unit, 1986: 46)

Training should encompass:
• The human side of the problem and the feelings of the victim.
• The need for accurate recording in incident report books.
• Good knowledge of legislation.
• Suggested reading list for trainers.
• Training for managers at sergeant and inspector level.
(Metropolitan Police Working Party, 1986: 56–8)

This list is by no means exhaustive, but includes the major reports covered during this study. These recommendations have been endorsed by many individual writers and researchers, and the volume of interest shown indicates the importance attached by them to this area of police work.

Although there are many calls on police time for all kinds of training, it is felt that some essential features must be covered in order to undo some of the myths and taboos which have become associated with marital violence.

Progress and the way forward

A more sympathetic and positive approach by the police to marital violence may, in the short term at least, give the appearance that marital violence has increased. In his Annual Report for 1988, the Commissioner of Police for the Metropolis makes reference to this trend as follows:

> The emphasis placed on follow-up visits and close contact with the victim, and increased confidence in police activity, have contributed to a rise of 42% in domestic violence incidents in 1988 over 1987, though the new guidelines were implemented only in June, 1987 and the figures are not strictly comparable.

The report goes on to comment that the total number of offences cleared up had risen by 83 per cent.

If this experience is duplicated elsewhere, it seems likely that domestic violence offences reported to the police will rise, at least in the short term. However, it must be recognized that this is a strength of the policy, not a weakness.

A further trend has been the formation of domestic violence units in a number of police areas throughout the country. The first of these was established in Tottenham and was described by Edwards (1989) as tackling the problem 'vigorously, sensitively and seriously'. The pilot scheme in Tottenham was extended to a further nine police divisions in London during 1988.

Constant reference has been made in this work to the pilot studies in Minneapolis and London, Ontario. The Minneapolis project has been replicated by the US Department of Justice in six other locations in the USA, on the basis that the apparent success of the Minneapolis scheme needs to be validated in a variety of differing locations and conditions, in order to test more fully the hypothesis that the arrest option is the one which has the greatest impact on potential re-offenders, and therefore is the best working practice.

The time seems to be ripe for a British police force to consider introducing a pilot scheme similar to those in North America. Smith (1989) advocates such a 'longitudinal study' in the Home Office Research and Planning Unit's own study of the problem. Although the British and American legal systems do not match exactly, the British system is sufficiently flexible to accommodate such a scheme, for all we are really discussing is invoking action in all cases of criminal injuries (actual bodily harm and above), for which police powers of arrest and prosecution already exist. As a counter to the anticipated claim that this policy would be likely to throw an unbearable burden on existing resources, the evidence of the Minneapolis scheme was that resources were eventually saved because of the reduction in the number of re-offenders.

To continue as we are has its attractions, but it also has its drawbacks. For as the groundswell of public opinion for action over this problem begins to mount, as for example in the case of the non-publication of the Metropolitan Police Working Party Report (1986), the British police system will continue to be seen to be lagging behind in its willingness to answer the needs of victims. It is unlikely that the police service will ever embrace the aspirations of the radical feminist movement, but it is likely to shift its ground away from the cautious negative line of the earlier police instructions, or the 'lesser of two evils' approach adopted by the ACPO in 1975, when giving evidence to the Parliamentary Select Committee.

Having known and worked with many police officers in a number of police forces for over 30 years, I am aware that the majority feel personally involved in the misery brought about in cases of marital violence. They see the hopelessness and indignity, and witness the injuries and pain that both the victims and their children suffer. Above all, some have attended homicides and suicides which have arisen from domestic situations. From the evidence gathered over the 4 years of this study, the impression is that the time is right for a change in attitude and policy, to bring about the justice which victims have the right to expect and for which the 'British Bobby' has always been renowned. The two key words on which the new approach should be based may be found in the title of the Commissioner's Report:

To Serve and Protect.

— References

Adler, M. and Asquith, S. (1979). *Discretion and Power.* University of Edinburgh Press, Edinburgh.

Alderson, J. (1980a). Policing a democratic society. *Vole*, November.

Alderson, J. (1980b). In *Course D335: Controversies around Police Powers and Accountability.* Open University Press, Milton Keynes.

Andrews, B. (1987). *Violence in Normal Homes.* Paper presented to the Marriage Research Centre Conference on Family Violence, 15 April.

Benyon, J. and Bourn, C. (eds) (1986). *The Police – Powers, Procedures and Proprieties.* Pergamon Press, Oxford.

Berg, B. L. and Budnick, K. J. (1986). Defeminization of women in law enforcement: A new twist in the traditional police personality. *Journal of Police Science and Administration*, **14**(4).

Binney, V., Harknell, G. and Nixon, J. (1981). *Leaving Violent Man.* National Women's Aid Federation, London.

Blackstone's Commentary on the Laws of England (1765).

Bottomley, J. (1973). In *The Police and the Law* (ed. J. Wegg-Prosser). Longman, London.

Bourlet, A. R. (1986). *Dialogue for Change.* Welsh Office, Cardiff.

Brewer, E. C. (1978). *The Dictionary of Phrase and Fable.* Avenal Books, New York.

Burris, C. A. and Jaffe, P. (1984). *Wife Battering – A Well Kept Secret. Canadian Journal of Criminology*, **2**, 171–7. University of Western Ontario Press.

The Chartered Institute of Public Finance and Accountancy (1987). *Police Statistics 1987–88 Estimates.* Reeds Ltd, Penrith.

Chatterton, M. (1981). *Report of the Royal Commission on Criminal Procedure.* HMSO, London.

Commissioner of Police for the Metropolis (1984). *Annual Report 1984.* Metropolitan Police, London.

Commissioner of Police for the Metropolis (1988). *Annual Report 1988.* Metropolitan Police, London.

Connors, J. (1987). *Confronting Violence.* Commonwealth Secretariat, London.

Critchley, T. (1978). *A History of the Police in England and Wales.* Constable, London.

Davis, K. C. (1971). *Discretionary Justice: A Preliminary Enquiry.* University of Illinois Press, Urbana, Illinois.

Department of Transport (1987). *Road Accident Statistics, Christmas 1987.* HMSO, London.

Dobash, R. E. and Dobash, R. P. (1979). *Violence Against Wives.* Open Books, Shepton Mallet.

Dobash, R. E., Dobash, R. P. and Cavannagh, K. (1985). Battered women and social and medical agencies. In *Private Violence and Public Policy* (ed. J. Pahl). Routledge and Kegan Paul, London.

Domestic Violence and Matrimonial Proceedings Act (1976). HMSO, London.

Domestic Proceedings and Magistrates' Courts Act (1978). HMSO, London.

Edwards, S. S. M. (1985a). *Protecting Victims of Family Violence.* Polytechnic of Central London, London.

Edwards, S. S. M. (1985b). *Remedying Violence Against Women.* Polytechnic of Central London, London.

Edwards, S. S. M. (1985c). *Protecting Women.* Polytechnic of Central London, London.

Edwards, S. S. M. (1986). *When is a Crime a "Crime"?: Domestic Violence and Policing in Central London.* Polytechnic of Central London, London.

Edwards, S. S. M. and Bourlet, A. R. (in prep.). *Report on Results of Questionnaires in Metropolitan Police and Kent Police on Marital Violence.*

Edwards, S. S. M. (1989). *Policing 'Domestic' Violence.* Sage, London.

English, J. (1986). *Police Training Manual.* McGraw-Hill, London.

Faragher, T. (1985). The police response to violence. In *Private Violence and Public Policy* (ed. J. Pahl). Routledge and Kegan Paul, London.

Freeman, M. D. A. (1987). *Dealing with Domestic Violence.* CCH Editions, Bicester.

GLC Police Committee (1986). *Policing London.* GLC Police Committee Support Unit, London.

Goldstein, H. (1963). Police discretion, the ideal v. the real. *Public Administration Review*, **23**, September.

Hanmer, J., Radford, J. and Stanko, E. A. (1989). *Women, Policing & Male Violence.* Routledge and Kegan Paul, London.

Home Office (1972). *Report of the Committee on Privacy* (the Younger Report). HMSO, London.

Home Office (1983). *Crime Statistics, England and Wales.* HMSO, London.

Home Office (1986a). *Police Initial Training Notes.* HMSO, London.

Home Office (1986b). *Report of Her Majesty's Chief Inspector of Constabulary for 1985.* HMSO, London.

Home Office (1989). *Report of Her Majesty's Chief Inspector of Constabulary for 1988.* HMSO, London.

Horley, S. (1988). Homing in on violence. *Police Review*, January.

House of Commons Parliamentary Select Committee (1976). *Report on Violence in Marriage*. HMSO, London.

House of Commons Select Committee on Violence in Marriage (1975). *First Special Report*. HMSO, London.

Hurd, D. (1987). *Keynote Speech to the Superintendents' Association of England and Wales*, 22 September. Official text. Home Office, London.

Jaffe, P., Thompson, J. and Wolfe, D. (1986). *The Family Consultant Service with the London Police Force*. Document prepared for the Ministry of the Solicitor General of Canada.

Johnson, N. (1985). *Marital Violence*. Routledge and Kegan Paul, London.

Kemp, H. and Kemp, R. (1978). *Child Abuse*. Fontana, London.

Kennedy, D. B. and Homant, R. J. (1983). Attitudes of abused women toward male and female police officers. *Criminal Justice and Behavior*, **10**(4).

Kiralfy, A. K. R. (1967). *The English Legal System*. Sweet and Maxwell, London.

London Strategic Policy Unit (1986). *Police Response to Domestic Violence*, Briefing Paper No. 1. Police Monitoring and Research Group, London.

MacLeod, L. (1980). *Wife Battering in Canada: The Vicious Circle*. Canadian Government Publishing Centre, Quebec.

Mark, R. (1977). *Policing a Perplexed Society*. Allen and Unwin, London.

Mark, R. (1979). *In the Office of Constable*. Fontana/Collins, London.

Matrimonial Homes Act (1983). HMSO, London.

McClintock, E. H. (1963). *Causes of Violence*. St Martins Press, New York.

MacGrath, S. (1986). *Memorandum to All Chiefs of Police*. Ontario Police Commission, Toronto.

Metropolitan Police Working Party (1986). *Report into Domestic Violence*. Metropolitan Police, London.

McConaghy, J. F. (1976). Police crisis intervention in domestic disputes. *Australian Police Journal*, July.

Montgomery, P. and Bell, V. (1986). *Police Response to Wife Assault*. Northern Ireland Women's Aid Federation, Belfast.

Offences Against the Person Act (1861). HMSO, London.

Oppenland, N. (1982). Coping or copping out. *Criminology*, November.

Oxford, K. (1986). The power to police effectively. In *The Police – Powers, Procedures and Proprieties* (eds J. Benyon and C. Bourn). Pergamon Press, Oxford.

Pagelow, M. D. (1981). *Woman Battering – Victims and Their Experiences*. Sage, Beverley Hills.

Pahl, J. (1978). *A Refuge for Battered Women*. HMSO, London.

Pahl, J. (1980). *A Bridge Over Troubled Waters*. DHSS, London.

Pahl, J. (1982). Police response to battered women. *Journal of Social Welfare Law*, November.

Pahl, J. (ed.) (1985a). *Private Violence and Public Policy*. Routledge and Kegan Paul, London.

Pahl, J. (1985b). Violence against women. In *Social Problems and Welfare Ideology* (ed. N. Manning). Gower, Aldershot.

Parker, S. (1985). The legal background. In *Private Violence and Public Policy* (ed. J. Pahl). Routledge and Kegan Paul, London.

Pizzey, E. and Shapiro, J. (1982). *Prone to Violence*. Hamlyn, London.

Police and Criminal Evidence Act (1984). HMSO, London.

Police Act (1964). HMSO, London.

Policy Studies Institute (1983). *Police and People in London*. Policy Studies Institute, Iver.

Regina v *Metropolitan Police Commissioner, ex parte Blackburn* (1968).

Reiner, R. (1981). Politics of Police Powers. In *Politics & Powers* (ed. M. Prial *et al.*) Routledge and Kegan Paul, London.

Reiner, R. (1985). *The Politics of the Police*. Harvester, Brighton.

Roy, M. (ed.) (1984). *Battered Women*. Van Nostrand Reinhold, New York.

Royal Commission on the Police (1962). *Report*. HMSO, London.

Scraton, P. (1982). In *Course D335: Controversies around Police Powers and Accountability*. Open University Press, Milton Keynes.

Sex Equality Act (1976). HMSO, London.

Shakespeare, W. (1975). *The Taming of the Shrew*. Avenal Books, London.

Sherman, L. W. and Berk, R. A. (1984). *Minneapolis Domestic Violence Experiment*. Police Foundation, Washington, D.C.

Smith, L. J. F. (1989). *Domestic Violence: An Overview of the Literature*. Home Office Research Study No. 107. HMSO, London.

South Wales Constabulary (1986a). *Information Resource Indicator System*. Unpublished statistics, Bridgend.

South Wales Constabulary (1986b). *Assaults on Police Officers – First Quarter 1986*. Unpublished statistics, Bridgend.

Stead, P. J. (1972). *The Police*. Sweet and Maxwell, London.

Taylor, C. C. (1986). *The Church and the Police*. Metropolitan Police, London.

Welsh Women's Aid (1985). *Annual Report 1984/85*. Fingerprints, Cardiff.

Welsh Women's Aid (1987). *Annual Report 1986/87*. Fingerprints, Cardiff.

Woman Magazine (1985). Special investigation. February.

Woman Magazine (1987). The way we are. Questionnaire, 27 June; Results, 14, 21 and 28 November.

Women's Aid Federation (1989). *Unhelpful Myths and Stereotypes about Domestic Violence*. Women's Aid Federation, London.

Women's National Commission (1985). *Violence Against Women – Report of an ad-hoc Working Group*. Cabinet Office, London.

Working Party on Police Probationer Training (1971). *Report* HMSO, London.

— Index

accountability, 19, 20
  political influences, 66–8
  public opinion and, 64–5
actual bodily harm, 5, 7, 9, 10, 40–1,
  45, 56, 86
Adler, M., 54
adultery, 8
advisory leaflets, 63
age range (women and partners), 38,
  39
alcohol, 44
Alderson, John, 14, 65
All Wales Conference (1986), 30, 76,
  93
Anderton, James 20, 55
Andrews, B., 38–9
arrest
  clauses, 9–10, 24, 79–80, 89–90
  option (impact), 59, 101
  powers, 9–10, 45, 67, 79, 89
Asquith, S., 54
Association of Chief Police Officers,
  14, 18, 21, 26–7, 51–2, 60, 85,
  89, 102
Australia, 85, 92

batterings
  first, 40–5, 50
  worst, 41–4, 50
Bell, V., 30, 100

Benyon, J., 53
Berg, B. L., 46
Berk, R. A., 59, 86
Binney, V., 3, 17, 25, 45, 46, 94
Bottomley, J., 22
Bourlet, Alan R., 56
Bourn, C., 53
breach of the peace, 19, 23, 76, 77,
  78, 79
Bristol City Police Instruction Book
  (1880), 15
British system, 85–7, 89, 101–2
Budnick, K. J., 46
Burris, C. A., 59
Byford, L., 25

Canada, 59, 84–6, 88, 92, 95, 101
Canterbury Women's Aid Refuge,
  33, 50
Cardiff Refuge, 33
career prospects, 22, 69
Chapman, Tracey, 96–7
charges (withdrawal of), 76, 78, 79
Chartered Institute of Public Finance
  and Accountancy, 66
Chatterton, M., 6, 76
Chesham, Lord, 52
chief constables, 14, 62–4, 98
  constitutional position, 51–4
chief officers, 51–6, 58, 64

chief officers (*cont.*)
  factors influencing change,
    64–70
  survey of policies, 34–5
children (effect of violent
    environment), 49–50
Chiswick Rescue Centre, 60
Citizen's Advice Bureaux, 81
civil law
  application of, 24–5
  enforcement, 79–80
civil remedies, 76, 77
Cleveland Child Abuse case, 99
code of conduct, 21–2, 34, 51
Colchester Study (1975), 7
Commissioner of Police for the
    Metropolis, 11, 20, 51, 64, 101
common assault, 5
common good, 23, 24
common law, 22, 24
Commonwealth Secretariat, 31, 84,
    89, 92
community relations, 64–5, 98
competing pressures
  background of study, 28–30
  international aspects, 31
  operational officers (attitudes and
    perceptions), 31–2
  questionnaire for victims, 32–4
  survey of Chief Officer policies,
    34–5
Computer Aided Dispatch, 95
computer data, 56, 62
conflict (sources), 42–5
Connors, J., 31, 84–5, 89–90, 92–3,
    96, 100
constables (constitutional position),
    53–4
control, 64
'cooling off' period, 76, 78–9
county court injunctions, 9, 10
courts (response of), 46, 50
crime reporting system, 72
criminal damage, 77

criminal law
  application of, 22–4
  enforcement, 76–9
'criming down', 5–6
crisis intervention, 28
Critchley, T., 23, 24
Crown Prosecution Service, 91

Daily Telegraph, 35
Davis, K. C., 19, 54, 63, 70
decision-making, 19, 34, 51
deferred decisions, 55, 76, 77
desertion for two years, 8
discipline, 21–2, 34, 51
discretion, 4, 27, 70
  competing pressures, 28, 29, 34
  good practice and, 62–3
  initiation of action and, 88–93
  police intervention and, 18–21
  policy implementation, 72, 73, 76,
    79
  policy making, 34, 54–6
'Discretionary Decision-Making', 19
divorce, 8
Dobash, R. E. and R. P., 1, 2, 3, 7,
    8, 15, 34, 36, 39, 42–4, 94
'domestic disputes', 21, 25, 29, 56, 71
Domestic Proceedings and
    Magistrates' Courts Act (1978),
    10, 58, 89
Domestic Violence and Matrimonial
    Proceedings Act (1976), 9–10,
    24, 58, 89
domestic violence units, 101
Dyfed Powis Police, 66

East Sussex Police Code (1900), 15
Edwards, S. S. M., 3, 6, 17, 29, 31–2,
    56, 72–3, 80–1, 88, 90, 96–7, 101
Enever v *the King* (1906), 53
enforcement of civil law, 79–80
enforcement of criminal law, 76–9
English, J., 17
entry, powers of 26, 84–5

exclusion orders, 8, 9–10
expectations (of victims), 93–4

'false powers and notions', 24, 26
family size, 38, 39
Faragher, T., 6, 26, 27, 29, 45
feminism, 28, 96, 102
first battering, 40–5, 50
Fisher v *Oldham Corporation*, 51, 53
follow-up visits, 101
force orders/instructions, 27, 29, 34,
    58–60, 86
Freeman, M. D. A., 67
future (implications for), 84–98
future (progress/way forward),
    99–102

gaming, 20, 55
Goldstein, H., 20
good practice, discretion and, 62–3
Graef, Roger, 64, 65, 92
Greater London Council, 25
Greater Manchester Police, 20
grievous bodily harm, 5, 40, 41, 45,
    86
Griffiths, Mr Justice, 53

Hanmer, J., 28, 29, 35
Hillsborough Football Stadium
    tragedy, 99
HM Chief Inspector of Constabulary,
    21, 25
HM Inspectors of Constabulary, 66,
    68
Homant, R. J., 46
Home Office, 21, 25, 34, 92
    Initial Training Notes, 17, 91, 94
    political influence of, 66, 67–8
    Research and Planning Unit, 101
    statistics, 6, 7, 10, 61–3, 95
    Younger Committee, 26
Home Secretary, 66–7
homicide, 10, 11, 63, 74, 75, 88
Horley, S., 3, 36, 49, 60

House of Commons select
    Committee on Violence in
    Marriage (1975), 2, 6, 10–14, 18,
    56, 62–3, 71, 85, 87, 89, 95, 100,
    102
House of Lords, 52
'human awareness skills', 93, 99
Hurd, Douglas, 64

immigration legislation, 100
implications of study, 84–98
incident report books, 72
injunctions, 8–10, 24, 45, 79–80,
    89–90, 95
injuries
    first battering, 40
    suffered by police, 18, 95
    worst battering, 41–2
'intent', 5
inter-generational pathology, 37
international aspects, 31, 84–5
interviews
    attitudes/perceptions of police,
    31–2
    of men, 39–40
    of women 38–9
irretrievable breakdown, 8
Isle of Man, 58

Jaffe, P., 59, 86
Jersey, 58
Johnson, N., 26
justices of the peace, 22, 23, 55

Kemp, H. and R., 37, 38
Kennedy, D. B., 46
Kent Police, 4, 18, 29–30, 72–3, 76,
    78–82, 99
Kiralfy, A. K. R., 23, 24

'learned' violence, 37, 38, 49
length of service (Kent officers),
    72–3
life-threatening incidents, 40, 45, 93

Liverpool City Police Instructions
(1926), 15, 85, 89
Llandrindod Wells Conference
(1986), 30, 76, 93
London Strategic Policy Unit, 69, 88,
100
longitudinal study, 101
Luton Refuge, 3

McClaren v *McClaren*, 10
McClintock, E. H., 7
McConaghy, J. F., 18
MacGrath, Shaun, 86
Macleod, L., 95
marital status (Kent officers), 72–3
marital violence, 96
    police perception of, 72–6
    policing at 'sharp end', 87–8
    reasons for, 42–5
marital violence (nature and extent)
    definitions, 1–2, 4–5
    nature of, 2–3
    official figures, 6–12
    police 'criming' in practice, 5–6
    police recording practice, 3–4
    under-reporting, 3
Mark, R., 25
Marriage Guidance, 81
Matrimonial Homes Act (1983), 89
Mayne, Sir Richard, 23, 24, 26
media campaigns, 64
medical examination, 68
medical treatment, 40, 41
men
    assault of (by women), 1–2
    interview of, 39–40
    why women stay with, 47–8
Metropolitan Police, 4, 21, 23, 60, 66,
72
    memo to Select Committee, 13
    policy making, 55, 56
    Working Party (1986), 29–30, 50,
    94, 95, 96, 100, 102
mineworkers' dispute (1984–5), 68

Minneapolis study, 59–60, 84, 86, 88,
101, 102
Montgomery, P., 30, 100
murder, 10, 11, 63, 74, 75, 88

National Association of Victim
    Support Schemes, 81
National Institute of Justice, 86
National Statistics, 63
non-arrest, 76, 77

Offences Against the Person Act
    (1861), 4–5, 40, 41
official figures, 6–12
Ontario, 59, 84, 86, 88, 101
Oppenland, N., 4, 17
'original authority', 19, 21, 72
Oxford, Kenneth, 53

Pagelow, M. D., 34
Pahl, J., 1, 3–4, 15, 17, 25–6, 29–30,
    36, 40, 46, 65, 70–1, 94
parental environment of victims, 37,
    38, 39–40, 49
Parker, S., 8, 9
Parliamentary Select Committee, 2,
    6, 10–14, 18, 56, 62–3, 71, 85,
    87, 89, 95, 100, 102
Peel, Sir Robert, 64, 82
personal factors (influencing change),
    69–70
personal protection order, 10
Pizzey, E., 37, 38, 46
police
    action, 45, 50
    attitudes and approaches, 98
    attitudes and perceptions, 31–2
    contact with (after first assault),
    44–5
    'criming down', 5–6
    as individuals, 22, 24–5, 54
    injuries sustained, 18, 95
    perception of marital violence,
    72–6

response (women's perception of),
    42, 96
systems and statistics, 94–7
women's attitudes to, 47, 50
Police Act (1964), 51, 52, 55, 56, 66
police authorities, 55, 68, 92
Police and Criminal Evidence Act
    (1984), 65, 67, 90
Police Grant, 66
police intervention, 13
    civil law, 24–5
    competing pressures, 28–35
    criminal law, 22–4
    discipline and, 21–2
    discretion, 18–21
    implications for the future, 84–98
    perception of own role, 14–18
    perception of role by others, 25–7
    progress and the way forward,
        99–102
police policy
    British system, 85–7
    Chief Officers survey, 34–5
    competing pressures, 28–35
    formulation, *see* policy formulation
    implementation, *see* policy
        implementation
    improvements (suggestions),
        99–102
police recording practice, 3–4
Police Review, 49
police role
    perceptions by others, 25–7
    perceptions by police, 14–18
Police Superintendents' Association of
    England and Wales, 64
police surgeon, 68
police systems and statistics, 94–7
Police Training Council, 92
policewomen, 33, 34, 46–7, 68
policing
    by consent, 64
    at sharp end, 87–8
    way forward, 99–102

policy formulation
    discretion and, 34, 54–6, 62–3
    factors influencing change, 64–70
    questionnaire, 56–62
    Royal Commission (1962), 51–4
policy implementation, 71
    enforcement, 76–80
    police perceptions and, 72–6
    social work, 80–3
Policy Studies Institute, 74
political influence, 66–8
pornography, 20, 55
powers
    of arrest, 9–10, 45, 67, 79, 89
    of entry, 26, 84–5
    false powers and notions, 24, 26
priorities, 51
    competing pressures, 28–35
    policing levels and, 20–1
privacy rights, 26
professional women, 39
progress (and the way forward),
    101–2
prosecutions, 6
    Crown Prosecution Service, 91
    influences on, 48–9
    withdrawn, 32, 76, 78–9, 87–90,
        97
prostitution, 20, 26, 55
protection orders, 10
public opinion, 64–5, 87, 102

Queen's Peace, 19, 22–3, 24, 52, 55
questionnaire
    Chief Police Officers, 35
    domestic violence policy, 56–62
    for victims, 32–4, 37–8

racism, 100
rape victims, 25, 26, 68
    Thames Valley documentry, 64,
        65, 92
'reciprocal training', 76
reconciliation, 48, 90

records
    official figures, 6–12
    police practice, 3–4
    statistical, 61–2
    under-recording, 3–4, 6, 11, 18, 56, 96
    under-reporting, 3, 6, 11, 56, 96
refuges, 25, 30, 33, 50, 93, 99
Reiner, R., 64, 73
Report of the Royal Commission on Criminal Procedure (1981), 76
Rochester project, 18, 72–3, 76, 78–82
role expectations, 94, 97–8
Rowan, Col. Sir Charles, 23, 24, 26
Royal Commission on Criminal Procedure (1981), 76
Royal Commission on the Police (1962), 19, 22, 51–4, 55, 72
Royal Ulster Constabulary, 30, 58
'rubbish', 73, 80–3

sanctions, 21, 34, 51
Scarman Tribunal, 65
Scraton, P., 19, 20, 54–5, 64, 66, 70
separation for five years, 8
separation or two years, 8
Sex Equality Act (1976), 92
sexism, 100
Shapiro, J., 37, 38, 46
Sherman, L. W., 59, 86
Smith, L. J. F., 101
social class, 39, 40, 82
social problems, 70
social service departments, 80–1, 83, 99
social work, 80–3
socio-economic group, 39, 40
South Wales Constabulary, 18, 21, 56, 95
special instructions, 100
specialized units, 92
Staffordshire Police, 26
station message books, 72

statistics
    official figures, 6–12
    police systems and, 94–7
    records, 61–2
    under-reporting, 3
Stead, P. J., 82
Stewart, James K., 86
'stitch rule', 6, 15
summonses, 63
supervisory officers, 18, 98
supportive regime, 96, 97

Taylor, C. C., 21
Thames Valley Police, 64, 65, 92
Tottenham pilot scheme, 101
training, 17, 74, 76, 92
    further, 60–1, 99
    human awareness skills, 93, 99
    need for, 100–1
Training Committee of the ACPO, 92

under-recording, 3–4, 6, 11, 18, 56, 96
under-reporting, 3, 6, 11, 56, 96
uniformed employment (husbands in), 82, 98
United States, 85
    Minneapolis study, 59–60, 84, 86, 88, 101, 102
unlawful wounding, 5
unreasonable behaviour, 8

value judgements, 79, 94, 97
victims
    interviews, 38–40
    questionnaires, 32–4, 37–8
    support schemes, 83
    wishes and expectations, 93–4
victims (expectations and needs), 36
    effect on children, 49
    first battering 40–5, 50
    police action, 45, 50
    prosecutions, 48–9

questionnaire and interviews,
37–40
reasons for violence, 42–5
response of courts, 46
why women stay, 47–8
wishes of victims, 46–7
women's attitudes to police, 47, 50
worst battering, 41–4, 50
violence, *see* marital violence

Wallis, Maria, 60
Welsh Office, 7, 30, 93
Welsh Women's Aid, 7, 30, 76, 83,
93
West Yorkshire study, 29
Woman Magazine surveys
(1985), 1, 2, 3, 11, 36, 82, 98
(1987), 36
women
assaults by, 1–2
attitudes to the police, 47
interview of, 38–9
perception of police response, 42
reasons for staying, 47–8

see also victims; victims
(expectations and needs)
Women's Aid, 80–1, 100
refuges, 25, 30, 33, 50, 93, 99
Welsh, 7, 30, 76, 83, 93
Women's Committee Support Unit
(GLC), 25–6
Women's Movement, 8
Women's national Commission
Report (1985), 3, 6, 11–12, 14,
18, 21, 27, 45, 54, 56, 62–4,
67–8, 88, 92, 95, 100
working class, 39, 82
Working Party on Domestic
Violence, 29–30, 50, 94–6, 100,
102
Working Party on Police Probationer
Training, 17, 74, 91
working practices, good, 62–3, 94
worst battering, 41–4, 50
woundings, 7, 41, 56

Yorkshire Ripper case, 99
Younger Committee, 26